Media Lab Books
For inquiries, call 646-838-6637

Copyright 2017 Topix Media Lab

Published by Topix Media Lab
14 Wall Street, Suite 4B
New York, NY 10005

Printed in China

ISBN 10: 1-942556-10-1
ISBN 13: 978-1-942556-10-7

CEO

CE PRESIDENT OF BRAND MARKETING
IRECTOR OF FINANCE
IRECTOR OF SALES AND NEW MARKETS
ANUFACTURING DIRECTOR Nancy Puskuldjian
NANCIAL ANALYST Matthew
RAND MARKETING ASSISTANT Taylor Hamilton

EDITOR-IN-CHIEF Jeff
CREATIVE DIRECTOR Steven Charny
PHOTO DIRECTOR DAVE WEISS
MANAGING EDITOR Courtney Kerrigan
SENIOR EDITORS Tim Baker, James Ellis

CONTENT EDITOR Trevor Courneen
CONTRIBUTING WRITERS Carlos Mejia
ILLUSTRATOR Nick Harran
ART DIRECTOR Susan Dazzo
ASSISTANT MANAGING EDITOR Holland Baker
PHOTO EDITOR Meg Reinhardt
SENIOR DESIGNER Michelle Lock
DESIGNER Danielle Santucci
PHOTO ASSISTANT Julia Pressman
ASSISTANT EDITORS Alicia Kort, Kaytie Norman
CO-FOUNDERS Bob Lee,

Photography Courtesy World Wrestling Entertainment, Inc.; Shutterstock

IS THIS MEMO
FROM THE DESK OF

DANIEL BRYAN

GENERAL MANAGER

SMACKDOWN LIVE

[ ] No [✓] YES!

FOREWORD

When I first heard that some renegade employee had gotten their hands on the WWE Book of Rules and decided to share it with the world, I couldn't keep a slight smirk from crossing my face. That may come as a surprise considering I'm now a figure of authority (still can't get used to that word…) in WWE. But even though I've stepped into this new role, I'm still a Superstar at heart—and that's why I can appreciate this act of rebellion.

In a lot of ways, my in-ring career was built on breaking the so-called "rules" of WWE. I came into the company with a lot of eyes on me—many of them for the wrong reasons. There weren't any written directives stating you couldn't be a vegan if you worked for WWE. And I'm pretty sure I never saw a mandate that all Superstars own a television. But given the way some people talked to me in those days, you'd think such rules did exist. Some people referred to me as the "small-fry indie guy" or a "B-plus player." Michael Cole simplified things and just called me a nerd (Hey, pot? It's kettle. Got a message for you...). But I knew it was up to me to make them eventually call me "champion," and I was gonna break, ignore or rewrite any rule necessary to make that happen.

I actually have my own personal history with the WWE Book of Rules. I first encountered it the same night I made my *Raw* debut. I was wandering around backstage, anxious about making a major impact, and decided to stop by catering for a quick kale fix when I saw this rather unusual-looking folder on a table in the corner of the room. As far as official rule books go, it wasn't at all what you'd expect. Rough around the edges and totally unlike anything else I'd seen in the production office or anywhere else backstage. I couldn't take my eyes off of it (kinda sounds like me, doesn't it?!). I knew the rule book was important, and I looked forward to one day making my own additions to its pages. Ironically, I'd figuratively throw the whole thing right out the window later that same night when I joined the rest of Nexus to take over *Raw*. Obviously, we all make mistakes.

After I cooled down and settled into the company a little bit, I'd seek out the Book of Rules backstage and flip through it. I have a tremendous respect for the rich history of WWE, and I recognize the importance of having some guidelines here and there. There are plenty of rules I agreed with immediately. I won my first world championship thanks to the decree that you can cash in a Money in the Bank contract at ANY TIME (sorry, Show!). Plus, the somewhat loose dress code for Superstars allowed me to wear some pretty awesome robes, jackets and T-shirts on my way to the ring. Oh, and there's no edict against marrying a fellow Superstar, whether you're a Bella Twin or Billy and Chuck. But, obviously, the "rules"—or rather, the people in charge of enforcing them—eventually became a huge obstacle in my career. That's when I started to break the ones I didn't agree with and, in some cases, make my own.

Once The Authority started screwing me out of the WWE Championship any time I got near it, the Book of Rules became my new best friend. Sometimes I would bring it out just to throw in their face whenever I felt they were being hypocrites going against the framing document of their own company. Other times I would use it to mess with them, either by defacing memos, rewriting rules behind their backs or by tearing out any ridiculous additions as soon as they'd make them (Hint: You won't find a rule in here that says "B-plus players cannot be WWE champion").

My favorite way to use the Book of Rules during this time, though, was as inspiration. I would look at all the ways someone like Stone Cold Steve Austin would turn these rules upside down in retaliation against everything Mr. McMahon tried to put him through, and I related completely. I didn't drive a beer truck into the arena and hose everyone down, but I think I got under Triple H's skin just as much when I led members of the WWE Universe into the ring for our "Occupy Raw" movement. Then I would come to a page and see a rule written by Mick Foley, and I'd think about how he became champion despite being a far cry from the "corporate-looking" Superstar they've always preferred. That solidified my decision to let my beard and my hair grow even wilder in my uphill battles against The Authority. I came to learn which rules would help me and which ones I should go ahead and ignore, and I had history on my side to back it all up. And look how it worked out! I went on to shatter the glass ceiling at *WrestleMania 30*, winning the WWE World Heavyweight Championship. I became the general manager of *Smackdown*. And I don't think I could've done those things had I not interpreted this Book of Rules for myself, rather than sheepishly obeying it (I'm not a sheep, I'm a goat!).

I think the main thing I've taken away from my experience with the WWE Book of Rules is that, in WWE, as in life, sometimes you have to make your own law. Write your own code, and stand by it. So, as a former champion, as a general manager and the right-hand man of Shane McMahon, do I support the decision of a WWE employee to steal and distribute this extremely confidential Book of Rules, essentially sticking it to the brass at Titan Tower?

I've got three words for you:

YES! YES! YES!

Daniel Bryan
General Manager
SmackDown Live

Once a rule breaker,
now a rule enforcer.
(But still cool)

A NOTE *from the* EDITOR:

Dear Reader,

What you're about to read—or rather, experience—is a living, breathing document that has been written, revised, reinterpreted and regretted throughout WWE history. Despite hearing rumblings about this rule book since my very first day with the company, I always figured it was merely a myth. My assumption for years was that this fabled "infinitely expanding book of rules" was just part of locker room lore, like the stories of Crash Holly beating Mark Henry in an arm wrestling match or that rumor about Boogeyman being the result of a Papa Shango hex gone wrong.

Then I found it.

It was *SummerSlam* weekend in Brooklyn, and I had been assigned to interview some of the Superstars for an upcoming project. As I was walking by a production truck on my way out of the Barclays Center, I nearly tripped over something lying on the asphalt. I looked down to see a timeworn manilla folder bursting at all edges with content, pages and pages and pages spilling out from the sides. At first I thought it was an early draft of another Mick Foley manuscript or possibly the archive of an underground WWE fanzine. But as I carefully gathered the scattered pages, I began to realize the truth.

It wasn't just a folder of documents—it looked like an artifact that had survived chaos, calamity and the Corporation. Maybe it had been there when Ricky "The Dragon" Steamboat beat Macho Man Randy Savage for the Intercontinental Championship at *WrestleMania III*. It's entirely possible it had been run over by a beer truck, a zamboni, a monster truck or maybe all three during the rebellious reign of "Stone Cold" Steve Austin. It was probably there when Brock Lesnar conquered Undertaker's streak at *WrestleMania 30*, as the whole folder is marked with faded soda stains that look like they came from a classic spit take. I knew exactly what I was holding in my hands. This was the WWE Book of Rules.

I couldn't stop looking at it. I am, after-all, a lifelong WWE fan who landed a dream job the day I was hired as an editor with the company. The 12-year-old kid in me (who's still rocking a Mankind mask and a J.O.B. Squad T-shirt) was begging me to just crack it open and see what this continuously growing WWE time capsule, essentially, had inside. So, I did. And once I started flipping through everything, well, let's just say I had a hard time not

After he defeated Shawn Michaels in an Intercontinental Championship match at WrestleMania IX, Tatanka tried to change the rule stipulation that titles don't change hands in the event of a win by countout. He was unsuccessful.

As WWE has evolved, so have its rules.
For example, Maybe one day there will be a rule against
conspiring with those in charge in order to win a championship.
Of course, the Authority does have a final say in which rules are adopted.

breaking out into a one-man "THIS IS AWESOME" chant in that parking lot.

The WWE Book of Rules is unlike any other collection of regulations you might see in a sports organization, which is only natural, as professional wrestling within WWE is unlike any sport anywhere in the world. The rules are not neatly typed, bound and coated in a swank leather cover. Many are scrawled on scrap paper, some are penned on paper towels, pieces of stationery, sticky notes and in one case, a police report.

Of course, this chaotic incarnation is not how this rule book was originally

In 1989 the Bushwhackers submitted a rule requiring all Superstars march to the ring while moving their arms up and down as though they're climbing a ladder. They were the only ones who chose to follow it.

the World Wide Wrestling Federation from his own father, Jess McMahon. Under McMahon Sr., the business as we know it today began to take shape, with consummate showmen like "Gorgeous" George, "Nature Boy" Buddy Rogers and the mighty Bruno Sammartino dominating both the ring and the airwaves. These were the prototypical Superstars, the larger-than-life personas that set the tone for the rulers of the ring we watch today. And, under McMahon's watchful eye, the rule book continued to expand.

When Vince's son, Vincent Kennedy McMahon, began his consolidation of the business, vacuuming up the territories and bringing them under the umbrella of what would become WWE, the book came with him and underwent its own consolidation. Mr. McMahon's transformation of WWE revolutionized the business, and the rules soon followed suit. Soon, the apparel of the Superstars became an area of concern for those in charge, with the vibrant, sometimes overly scanty, very often outlandish outfits requiring new rules be written. Then the pageantry of Superstar entrances blossomed, leading to new standards being set for the right and wrong ways of going to and from the ring. And then came the Attitude Era, where the rule book may as well have been thrown out the window. In some ways, it was. But the interested parties at Titan Tower tried their best to keep things under control by vastly expanding the previously sparse directives for special stipulation matches and the manner in which Superstars conduct themselves. Unsurprisingly, the rich history and unpredictable nature of this company birthed the monstrous manilla folder of haphazard documents now considered the official WWE Book of Rules—a reference accessible by any Superstar and amended at will as circumstances required.

intended to come together. In the earliest days of WWE, the dos and don'ts were mostly limited to the action in the ring, with simple standards and practices for traditional matches.

Back in the days of the territories, the rule book supposedly traveled with the Superstars from town to town. Riding shotgun with the men who would define the business, it wound its way through the backroads of America, from Amarillo to Portland, from dusty barn to smoky sportatorium. Along the way, new rules were added, old ones rewritten and the unspoken laws of the business began to take shape. Rules were officialized on typewriters and the pages were presented to the Superstars of the past to be memorized and, hopefully, obeyed. But inevitably, those rules were bent and broken by brazen competitors in no time, leading to numerous new rules being created for not just the squared circle, but for all walks of life as a WWE Superstar.

In the early days of the business, the New York territory was overseen by Vince McMahon Sr., who had inherited

Just like any verbal decree or proclamation that takes place on WWE television, essentially none of these rules go unchallenged. No matter how old or new a rule is, there are always those who strongly object. It doesn't matter if it came from a Superstar or the Chairman himself—someone always has something to say in response, and they'll gladly deface the original rule to make their message known.

And because I simply couldn't keep this incredible secret to myself, I decided to go rogue and share it with the world. With the overflowing folder in hand, I ran to the nearest office supply store to scan as many copies as I could. Yeah, it was quite a task. A costly one, too (everybody does indeed have a price, Mr. DiBiase). So, I didn't quite get everything, but this is at least a vast representation of the mayhem that is this rule book. And as you'll see, anything can happen in WWE—even if the rules say otherwise.

Will I lose my job over this?
Probably.

Will it have been worth it?
See for yourself.

—The Anonymous *Raw* General Editor

RULE CATEGORIES

RULES OF THE RING
The middle of the arena is the center of the WWE Universe, which is why the commandments for competition had to be set early on. But even the oldest, most sacred rules are routinely ignored.

WHAT TO WEAR
While many Superstars have gone the route of traditional trunks, others have over-accessorized or, in some cases, underdressed in alarming fashion. Naturally, codes for dress became essential.

ENTRANCES AND EXITS
The seemingly simple process of traveling to and from a match has proven to be anything but in WWE. These regulations highlight the right and wrong ways to arrive and depart.

STIPULATION MATCHES
When a standard contest could no longer settle the score, the WWE brass decided to allow some rules to be set aside for special occasions. These are their attempts to control the chaos.

SUPERSTAR CONDUCT
The ideal WWE Superstar is not only a stellar athlete; they're a stand-up citizen and consummate professional. But as these rules show, many Superstars break the mold (among other things).

The earliest decrees in WWE history are found within the regulations governing competition. Of course, as countless Superstars have demonstrated, these rules are also the most unabashedly broken.

THE MOST STYLIN', PROFILIN' WAY TO FLY OUT OF THE RING.

RULES OF THE RING

MR. WRESTLEMANIA LIVING UP TO HIS NAME.

MURPHY - AND D- RELATED TO THE BOSS!

EVEN BROOKLYN BRAWLER CAN WIN A MATCH!

ANYTHING CAN happen

a one-legged man can become a superstar!

A leprechaun can

EVEN A VEGAN CAN BECOME A WWE WORLD HEAVYWEIGHT CHAMPION!

Great

The Ring Bell

Matches officially begin
and end with the ringing
of the bell

YES

It's also
a reliable
face rearranger
if a match is
getting out
of hand.

NO

Yeah. Just Ask
Cody Rhodes.

↰ You Mean
Stardust?

November 9, 1997

Attention All Officials:

When calling tonight's contests, please consider this, as you always should, THE GOLDEN RULE. Please also remember that while you are an authority figure, the CHAIRMAN always has the final say...especially during a main event contest for the championship.

—VKM

P.S. Fans in Montreal are known to be hostile, so please make note of all nearby security personnel.

Dictated not read

VINCE

BRET SCREWED BRET

VINCE

WCW

At the end of the day, the match comes down to you and the guy or gal in front of you. Who's got what it tak...

Falls

and streaks are Conquered!
—Heyman

Pinfalls occur when a Superstar pins their opponents to
the mat for a count of 3.

Pins can be broken if the
pinned Superstar is able to
lift their shoulder before a
count of 3, touch the rope
or if any part of their body
is under the ropes.

If a double pin results in a
3 count, the match is a draw.

Submissions

Submissions occur when a
Superstar verbally submits
or taps out. *OR WHEN RUSEV CRUSH*

Submission holds are broken
when a Superstar reaches
the ropes for a rope break.

NOTE: IGNORE ALL THESE RULES IF THE REF AIN'T WATCHIN'

DISQUALIFICATIONS

If a Superstar is disqualified, their opponent is
declared the winner.

Outside interference is
grounds for disqualification.

If a Superstar uses a
foreign object, they will
be disqualified.

Foreign?! My cast was made in America! —Cowboy Bob

Assaulting a referee in any
manner will result in a
disqualification.

Not if it's an "accident"...

Not always true...

When the action spills outside the ring, Superstars
have until the count of 10
to return to the ring or
they will be counted out/
disqualified.

If a Superstar reaches the
ropes during a submission,
their opponent has until
the count of 5 to break the
hold or they will be dis-
qualified.

What if they're not wearing a belt?

WOOOOOO!

Hitting below the belt will
result in a disqualification.

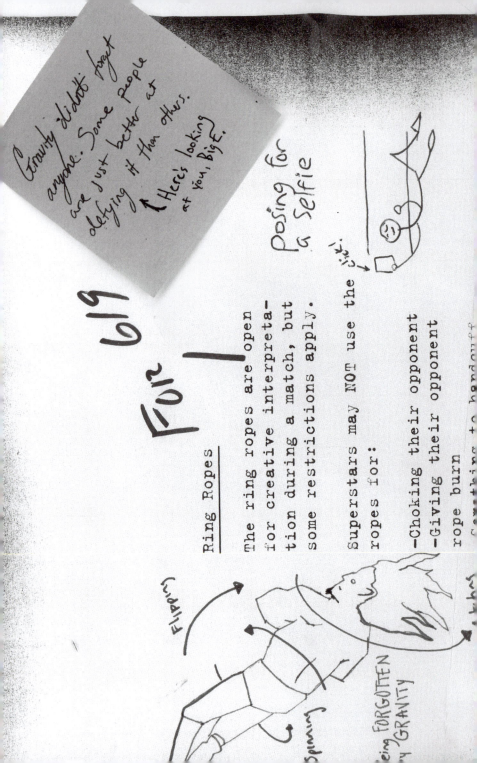

Gravity didn't forget anyone. Some people are just better at defying it than others.

↑ Here's looking at you, BigE.

For 619

Posing for a selfie

Ring Ropes

The ring ropes are open for creative interpretation during a match, but some restrictions apply.

Superstars may NOT use the ropes for:

- Choking their opponent
- Giving their opponent rope burn
- Something to handcuff

Posing for a selfie ← the dirt!

FLipping

SPinning

...being FORGOTTEN by GRAVITY

Championship Matches

During a championship match, the title can only change hands via pinfall or submission (unless indicated by special stipulations). The champion will technically lose the match if they are counted out or disqualified, but they will retain the title.

Just because a champion is competing in a match does not mean the championship is on the line. A title match must be indicated prior to the first bell ringing for fair notice.

Championship titles may not be used as weapons at any point during a match contested under standard rules. The title is to be kept in the timekeeper's area for the duration of the match.

If a champion is injured and will be sidelined for an extended period, they must forfeit their title.

Note to self:
DQ isn't always bad.

Consider this
"Fair Notice"
Edge

REDESIGN
REBUILD
RECLAIM
-SR

The 30-Day Clause

A reigning champion must defend their title at least once every 30 days, whether it be during a televised or non-televised event.

WWE STUDIOS
INVITES YOU TO THE MULTIMEDIA SCREENING OF:

THE MARINE 4
MOVING ★ TARGET

FRIDAY, APRIL 10, 2015
THE GROVE
189 The Grove Drive
(3rd Street at Fairfax Avenue)
Los Angeles, CA
DOORS OPEN: 5:45 PM — SCREENING STARTS: 6:30 PM

ADMIT ONE

...ions are strictly non-transferable and remain the property of WWE Studios. NO RECORDING ALLOWED.

Really?! Really?!
I am an A-LISTER.
I have RED CARPETS
to walk. I'll defend
this title when I
find time in my
HOLLYWOOD SCHEDULE

2 rows
8 rings

16 stones
each side

3.27"

3.08"

9.21"

inside track

WWE
Champion

3 every
other one
side

connected to
ring

W

Free
Spinning

stones

blake

raised
0.2"

track

magnet?

more individual
= more weigh

THE CHAMP CAN CUSTOMIZE HIS TITLE ANY WAY HE WANTS.

b: John Cena "Spinner Belt"

rap Dimensions: 55.9" x 10.43" x 0.2"

ight: 2.68 pounds.

55.9"

SMACK
DOWN
(slab)

4.19"

eagle

eagle

k eagle

stones

MAIN
plate

18 x 2
sq.
stones

3p

34 6mm

CHAMP

110
stones

slab serif

gold plate

side plate: 4.82" x 4.19"

side plate: 3.27" x 3.03"

thickness: .79" (main)   .28" (side)

WHAT ABOUT THE TELEVISION CHAMPIONSHIP?

Custom Titles

Provided they have the
means and skills to protect
it, a Superstar can create
their own championship.

A championship
should look
like a Million
bucks! HAHH
The Million
Dollar Man
Ted DiBiase

INTERNET CHAMPION

The skills AND the
means—You know it,
BRO!

Twitter @ZackRyder
YouTube LongIslandIcedZ

@ ZACK RYDER

one handsome bro!
Thanks bro!
no problem bro!

You need
friends, Zack.

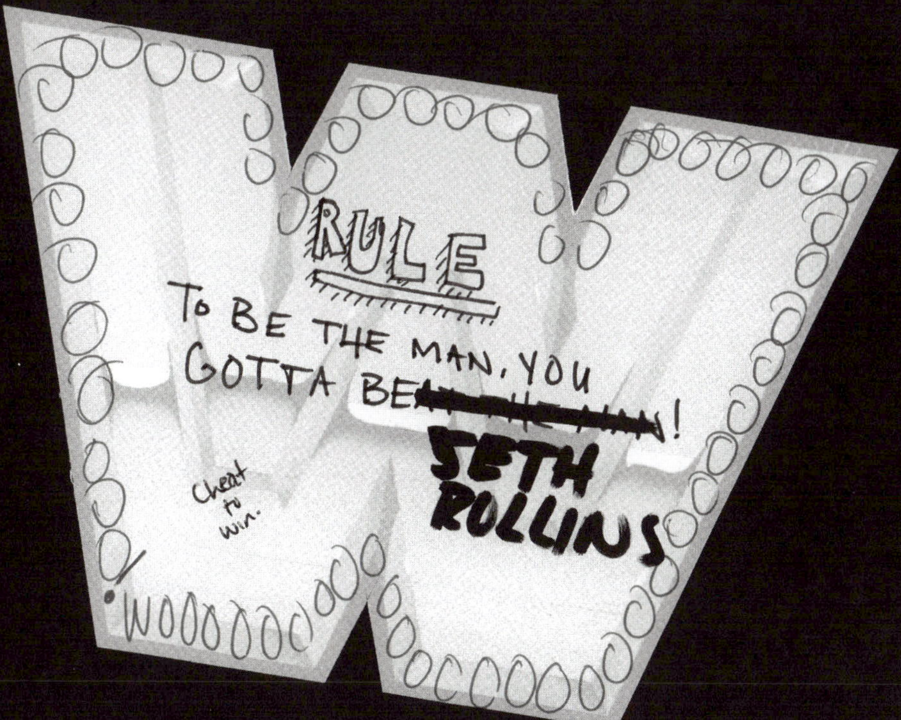

Unless you enjoy betrayal, don't align yourself with Triple H,

↑ or Seth Rollins

...about what a Cesaro twirl

three, even dizzying. I'm still queasy...

is so

It's true, he tried to do
his signature
was more like
BARK!
signature
but it
-Darren

Refs,

A puke bucket shoul
be kept at ringside during

has I'm embarrassed

FOOD IN THE RING
WILL ALMOST
ALWAYS END UP
ON SOMEONE'S
FACE. PLAN YOUR
LUNCHES
ACCORDINGLY.

A finishing Maneuver
Should have an
awesome memorable name...

POW! RIGHT IN
THE KISSER!

The Heartbreak Kid's
CHIN-BREAK-KICK

Super-DUPER KICK

PRETTY JAW SONG
almost.

If you
look closely
you can see
little pieces
of Ric Flair's
career.

Tag Team Matches

Best match for a main event, playa!

A standard tag team contest begins with one member of each team in the ring. The partners of each starting Superstar must wait on a designated area of the ring apron until they are tagged in.

While on the apron, a superstar cannot roam freely in order to reach their partner for a tag. They must hold onto the tag rope attached to the turnbuckle in order for a tag to count.

After a tag occurs the participants have a five count to make the switch, before they are disqualified.

The legal Superstar is the one who is currently tagged into the match. In moments of perilous pins and submissions, the legal Superstar may be rescued by their partner, but only one save is permitted for each team.

That's plenty of time to tell D-Von to GET THE TABLES!

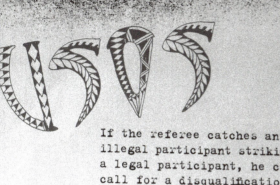

If the referee catches an
illegal participant striking
a legal participant, he can
call for a disqualification.

DO NOT allow Big show to do this. His hands are the size of FRYING PANS!

The high-five style is the
most typical type of tag,
but it is not required.
"Blind tags," which are often a surprise slap on the
back, are fair game.

Tornado Clause

For certain specialty
matches, the tag team cham-
pionships can be defend-
ed with tornado tag rules.
Originally known as a Texas
Tornado match, this stipulation allows for all members of both teams to be in
the ring at all times without tagging.

Big "Frying Pan Hands" Show

lol

Matt Hardy has slapped one of these.

I THOUGHT HE SLAPPED A TOMATO...

WEEEELLLL!

WORLD WRESTLING ENTERTAINMENT, INC.
1241 East Main Street, Stamford, CT 06902

October 1, 2012

Attention All Superstars,

In the event that you and a partner win the WWE Tag Team Championship, BOTH you and your partner would henceforth be champions. There has been some debate about this recently, so we wanted to address the issue before it escalated further.

Sincerely,
Talent Relations

I'm the Tag Team Champions!

NO. I'M THE TACT TEAM CHAMPIONS!

Gentlemen,
It seems we still have
some work to do...
Dr. Shelby

THE
ATLANTA
INN

If at first you don't succeed, try, try again. Or team up w/ a bunch of guys and take over.

THE FREEBIRD RULE

Teams of

3 or more fabulous members can choose any

What about the Nexus rule? You mess with any member you'll face all of them?

2 members for tag team championship defenses
—Michael "P.S." Hayes

OHHHHHH to not do so would be very, very BOOTY!

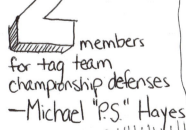

WORLD WRESTLING ENTERTAINMENT, INC.
1241 East Main Street, Stamford, CT 06902

Attention All Commentary Teams:

Commentators should remain impartial at all times, observing the action and providing insight o
for the viewers at home.

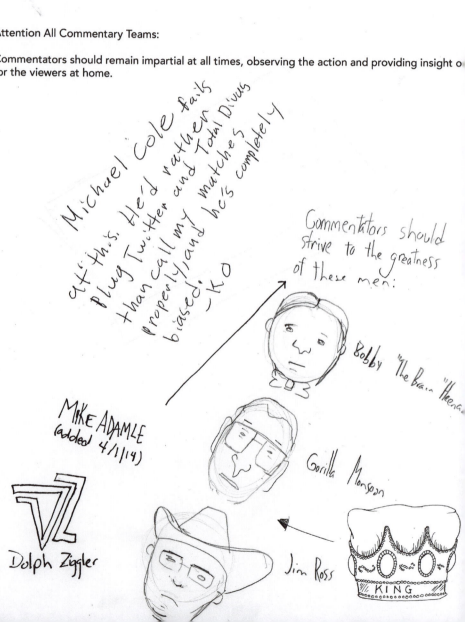

Michael Cole fails at this. He'd rather plug Twitter and Total Divas than call my matches properly, and bc is completely biased. -KO

Commentators should strive to the greatness of these men:

Bobby "The Brain" Heena

Gorilla Monsoon

MIKE ADAMLE
(added 4/1/14)

Dolph Ziggler

Jim Ross

KING

WWEMAIL

Acceptable Phrases
I message

Anonymous RAW GM <anonymousrawgm@wwe.com>
To: Michael Cole <michaelcole@wwe.com>

The following are acceptable exclamatory phrases for commentators:
- "WHAT A MANEUVER!"
- "BUSINESS JUST PICKED UP!"
- "YOU GOTTA BE KIDDING ME!"
- "VINTAGE!"
- "WILL YOU BE SERIOUS?"
* - "AND I QUOTE!"
- "SOMEBODY STOP THE DAMN MATCH!"

Commentators should refrain from creating their own isolated booth.

LURKIN IN A COLE MINE

The turnbuckle padding is for safety purposes. Please DO NOT eat it—even if you are an "Animal."

I won't eat it, but I will remove it behind the ref's back!

.: FREE :.
ADVICE

You don't need an umbrella when you meet Gorilla Monsoon.

A REFEREE'S REFERENCE
FOR REFEREEING
by a former referee

NOTE: EVEN IF YOU ARE MIKE TYSON, YOU SHOULD READ THIS...

Hello! If you're reading this, that means you've recently been hired as a WWE official (or you're serving as a special guest referee). While you've likely been briefed on what to expect when you're officiating, I'm here to help you prepare for some of the stuff only a former ref would know to look out for. So before you don the stripes, I suggest you consult the following list of dos and don'ts:

DO
purposely

-*Recover as quickly as you can if ~~inadvertently~~ knocked down.*
-*Have eyes in the back of your head.*
-*Check Tajiri's mouth for illegal green mist.*
-*Enforce the rules no matter how intimidating the competitors are.* *Until Undertaker looks you in the eyes...*
-*Make sure you have backup if breaking up a brawl.*

— Whatever the Authority ~~says~~ Scott

DON'T
or Lara's Beauty

-*Get distracted by managers/valets/tag partners.*
-*Allow William Regal to begin a match without patting him down first.*
-*Trade referee outfits with Shawn Michaels.*

-*Assume the correct Bella Twin is in the ring.*

-*Ask Cena if he gives up. (WASTE OF TIME)*

AND IF YOU GET KNOCKED OUT, HOPE TO GOD THERE'S A BACKUP REF AVAILABLE

Ringside Assistants

Superstars may be accompanied by the following types of individuals at ringside, so long as they do not interfere with matches in any way, shape or form:

Coaches/managers
Parents ~No, please don't let my momma embarass me...~ —Shelton
Siblings
Spouses/significant others
Tag team/stable partners

- Movie Stars

· Pro Athletes

- HEAVY METAL MUSICIANS

— Advocates

· STUNT DOUBLES!

Woooo!

But you BETTER KEEP YOUR EYES OFF ELIZABETH DIG IT?!

If you wanna succeed in this business, seek the services of one of these guys:

Ladies and
gentlemen,
my name is
PAUL HEYMAN

Advocate,
the
ONE Behind
the '21-1'

JIMMY HAR
RID
EX
M

"THE MOUTH *of the* SOUTH"

Yell into a megaphone, I'
yell back with mine at m
earliest convenience.

contact:

WORLD WRESTLING ENTERTAINMENT, INC.
1241 East Main Street, Stamford, CT 06902

Dear Superstars,

During competition, please do your best to remain inside the ring.

If you find yourself outside of the ring, either of your own volition or because you were unceremoniously tossed over the ropes, please refrain from searching beneath the ring apron for tools, ladders, tables or other "equalizers" to bring back into the ring with you. *or leprechauns!!!*

Obviously because the above requests are flouted so repeatedly, we ask that IF you are going to search beneath the ring apron that you PLEASE return it back to its proper position. The crew spends a lot of time making the ring look spectacular for television and live-audiences alike. No one wants to see a ring apron tossed haphazardly into the competition area.

Plus, you could slip on it which could be more debilitating than a sledgehammer to the gut.

Remember: Safety first.

—Talent Relations

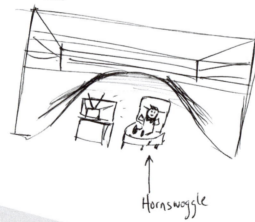

Hornswoggle

I feel like he's not the only Superstar living down the

12/09
Please be advised that the underside of the ring is not to be used as a court of law, for little people or anyone else. Ever again.

WHILE NOT A REQUIREMENT, ADDING "BIG" TO YOUR NAME IS A GOOD WAY OF HELPING PEOPLE REALIZE YOU ARE, IN FACT, LARGE. This does not apply in the case of Big Dick Johnson. In that case, 'Big' is just a synonym for 'Disgusting.'

EXAMPLES:

BIG SHOW

BIG CASS

BIG E

BIG BOSS MAN

BIG JOHN STUDD

BIG DADDY V

"BIG CAT" ERNIE LADD

BIG ANDRE THE GIANT

NXT IS GLORIOUS!

that means no one wants you on their show...

HAHA YOU'RE ON THE BLUE BRAND

Everything!

All Hea

We're

M. Monde

FROM THE DESK OF

VINCENT K. McMAHON

TITAN TOWER

July 19, 2016

Attention Superstars, *SMACKDOWN LIVE!*

As a reminder, the rules of the WWE Draft strictly prohibit Superstars from appearing on the opposing brand's programming. You are only to compete for the brand you have been drafted to.

NO EXCEPTIONS.

—VKM

RAW RULES!

But if you're not drafted, that means you're the HOTTEST FREE AGENT AROUND. BAY-BAY!

Aesthetic expression is a
major aspect of being
a WWE Superstar. But
while some have styled and
profiled with class, others
have strayed a bit off the
beaten path. These rules
are an attempt to
normalize the abnormal
whenever possible.

WHAT TO WEAR

If your second breathing fire is the coolest part of your entrance your outfit is on point.

Ring Gear

All in-ring gear can be
adorned with Superstar
names, team/faction names,
nicknames, logos, catch-
phrases, flags and designs
of any kind.

Traditional Gear:

Singlet   Trunks   Tights

Business Formal Wear

Jeans/tank top

← Please wash your tank-top, Harper

AIRBRUSH ADDEND

IN-RING GEAR CAN
ENRICHED WITH THE MAJO
OF AIRBRUSH LETTERING AN
DESIGNS. ALL ACCEPTABLE FOR
OF AIRBRUSH INCLUDE:
· NAMES
· NICKNAMES
· PHRASES
· NUMBERS
· ANIMALS
AND VARIOUS DESIGNS
↑
and opponents
spouses!

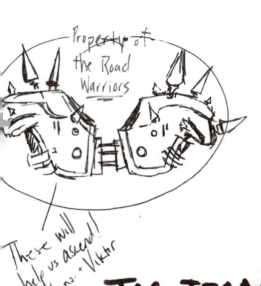

Property of
the Road
Warriors

These will
help us ascend!
—Konnor + Viktor

HART
FOUNDATION

↑
THE FOUNDATION
OF OUR SUCCESS

TAG TEAMS WHO ACCESSORIZE TOGETHER ARE MORE LIKELY TO :SUCCEED:

PEEPS
KNOW
HUGE
HATS
RULE!

New...
Day Rocks!

THE ROCK DOESN'T NEED YOUR PERMISSION, JABRONI!

GIVE 'EM TO THE KIDS

Sunglasses

Sunglasses can be worn to the ring, but should not be worn during matches.

OHHHH YEAHHH!

how to look legit

I look great in these. Deal with it

You can wear nearly anything
to get the drop on
your opponent:

- Druid
- Cameraman
- Santa Claus
- Mariachi Band Member ~~THERE'S ONLY ONE~~ GOLDUST.
- Doink the Clown
- Goldust Makeup / GOLDUST.
- Member of the WWE Universe
- The San Diego Chicken
- Gobbledy Gooker
- An Unknown Luchador

Brainstorm New Ideas:

- a wrapped birthday present

- SHEEP MASK
— A giant box of Booty-O's
- A NON-DOINK CLOWN?

IF YOU'RE LOSING YOUR HAIR,
EMBRACE BALDNESS BY
SHAVING YOUR HEAD

HAIR

= =

STUNNING
STEVE

STONE
COLD
STEVE

SUCCE

Add goatee
for bonus
badassery?

note:

wearing a bandana 24/7 doesn't fool anybody

A steel chain is not a foreign object! It's a fashion accessory!

Agreed, this is basic Thuganomics. ←

Trust him, He's a doctor.

Footwear

Regulation wrestling boots
are the only style of foot-
wear that is permissible
for the ring.

Furry tassels
make a
GORGEOUS
addition.

BANZAI!

these kicks
are money!
-Shane O'Mac

Attention Superstars,

While we support a champion's right to express him or herself, we ask that you adhere to one of the following ways to wear a championship title:

Around the waist

These belts are MASSIVE!

Over the shoulder (either)

PEOPLE'S CHAMP

Carried by your manager/mentor/advocate/tag team partner

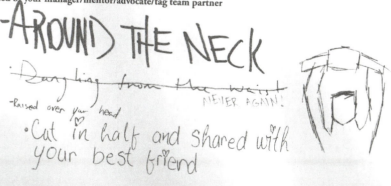

-AROUND THE NECK

~~Dangling from the waist~~ NEVER AGAIN!

-Raised over your head

• Cut in half and shared with your best friend

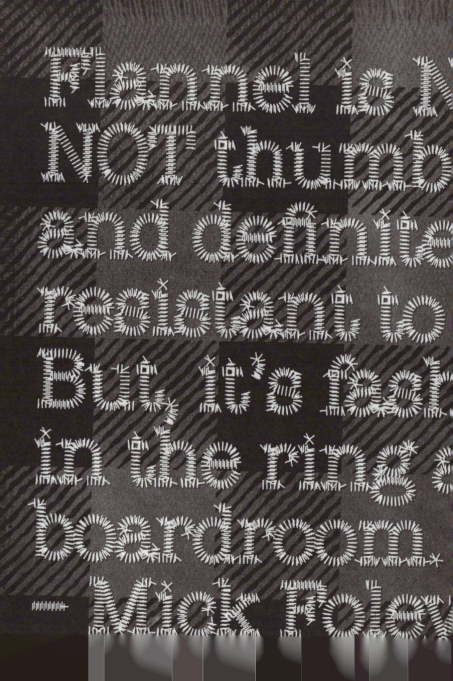

Flannel is N
NOT thumb
and definite
resistant to
But it's bet
in the ring c
boardroom
—Mick Foley

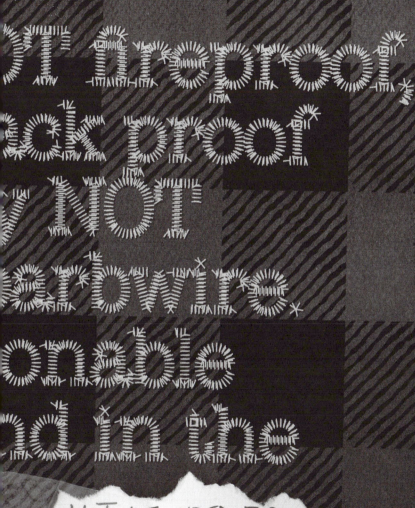

ot preproof,
ck proof
NOT
prowire,
onable
d in the

NOT REQUIRED FOR
LUMBERJACK MATCHES

Clothing Stipulation Matches

All clothing stipulation
matches require Superstars
to wear (or not wear) the
garments specified until they
reach the locker room.

Examples:

Crybaby Match — Baby ~~powder~~ is not necessary

Weasel Suit Match

Tuxedo Match

~~Bra Panties~~

Right to censor us here

-EVENING GOWN

This match a-make-a me so anger! Cobra too!

1-2-3 ~~KID~~ BABY

WAAAAHHH, I WOST TO WAZOR WAMON!!

Hey YO, check it out.

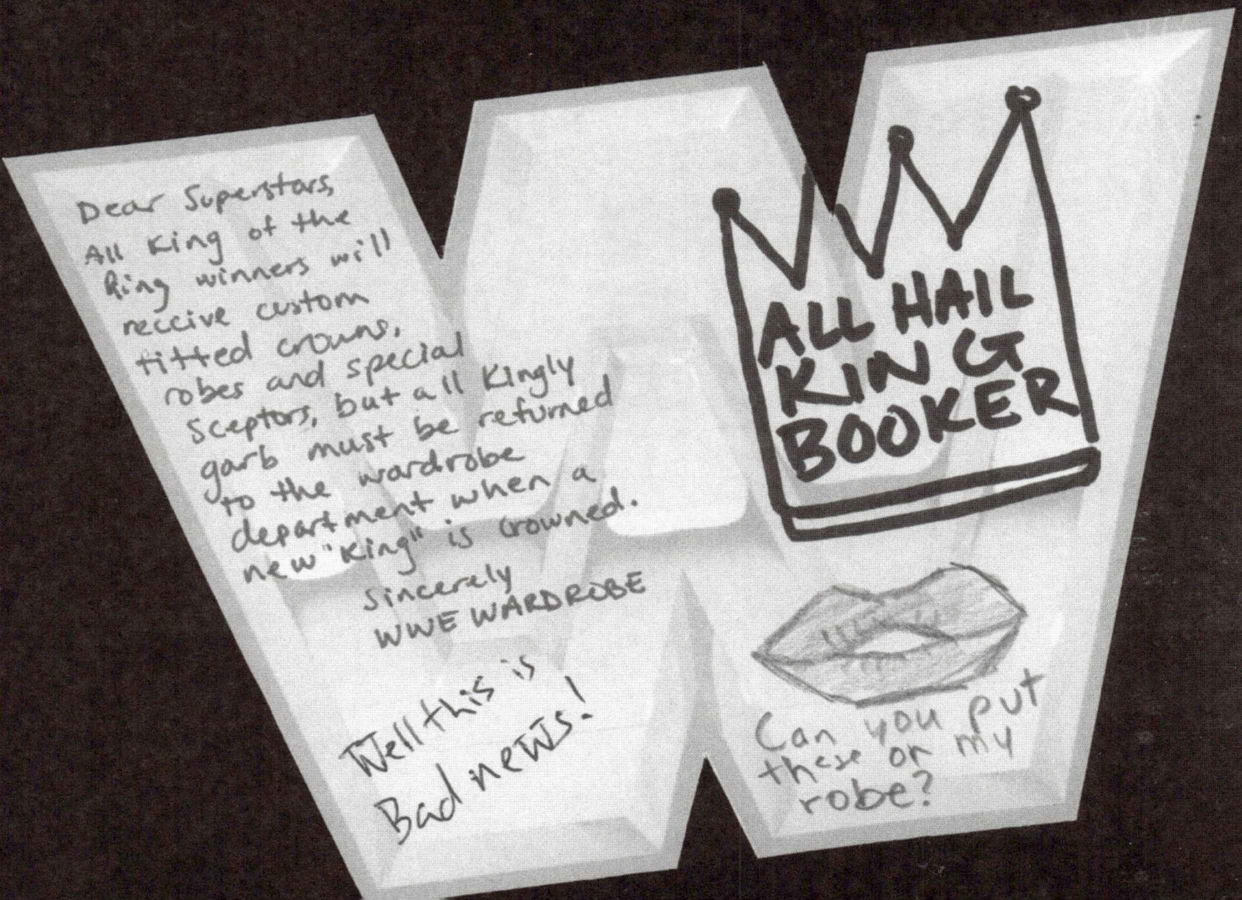

Dear Superstars,
All King of the Ring winners will receive custom fitted crowns, robes and special sceptors, but all kingly garb must be returned to the wardrobe department when a new king is crowned.

Sincerely
WWE WARDROBE

Well this is Bad news!

ALL HAIL KING BOOKER

Can you put these on my robe?

WORLD WRESTLING ENTERTAINMENT, INC.
1241 East Main Street, Stamford, CT 06902

Attention Wardrobe Department,

When crafting Superstar robes, please be sure to include at least TWO of the following elements for maximum effe

- Feathers ————————— *Please don't pluck from the Gobbledy Gooker*
- Superstar name, nickname or initials stitched in cursive
- Sparkles/Sequins
- Two colors (minimum)
- Wings ————— *Again, not from the Gobbledy Gooker*
- Tassels
- Hoods
- No sleeves

Best,
Talent Relations

OHHHH
YEAHHH!

CAROLINA CLEANERS

NAME: FLAIR, RIC				DATE: 3/28				
CALL	BY	MON.	TUES.	WED.	THURS.	FRI.	SAT. ✓	SUN.

QTY	DESCRIPTION					PRICE
	ROBES					
1	RED, SEQUINED W/ STITCHING					18.50
1	BLUE, FEATHERED, SILVER CAPE/ WINGS ON SLEEVES					25.50
1	GOLD, BEJEWELED W/STITCHING					18.50
	SHIRTS					
2	WHITE, LONGSLEEVE					10.50
	TROUSERS					
2	PLEATED KHAKIS					9.75
	MEN'S JACKETS					
1	BLACK					14.00
1	GRAY					14.00
	NOTES:					
	REMOVE "ELBOW DROP" IMPRINTS.					

YOU CAN NEVER LOOK TOO GOOD WHEN YOU'RE THEE MAN!

0001045   WOOOOOOOOO! | TOTAL | 110.75

NOT RESPONSIBLE FOR GOODS LEFT OVER 30 DAYS

Daddy, can I borrow this for my 'Mania match?

Masks

Masked Superstars are not
required to remove their
masks for official wrestling
license photos.

Probably a good idea for driver's licences though...

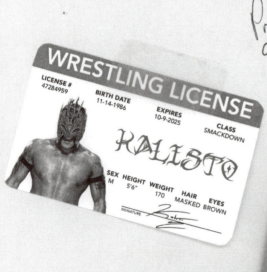

WRESTLING LICENSE

LICENSE #
47284959

BIRTH DATE
11-14-1986

EXPIRES
10-9-2025

CLASS
SMACKDOWN

KALISTO

SEX HEIGHT WEIGHT HAIR EYES
M   5'6"   170   MASKED BROWN

SIGNATURE

*If someone challe[nges]
you to put your mas[k]
on the line, make [sure]
sure they put someth[ing]
up, too (hair, champions[hip]
career, a large sum of $[,]
stamp collection, etc.)*

HEADWEAR
HALL OF FAME

THESE ITEMS ARE SO LEGENDARY, THEY SHOULD NEVER BE
REPLICATED OR WORN BY CURRENT OR FUTURE SUPERSTARS.

who would ever wanna wear that again?

IMPOSTERS
BEWARE

Um, whose is this?

**BY GAWD,
THAT'S MY HAT!**

THAT IS THE HAT OF A
WRESTLING GOD!

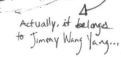

Actually, it belongs
to Jimmy Wang Yang...

Superstars can wear their hair however they see fit. **Styles** include:

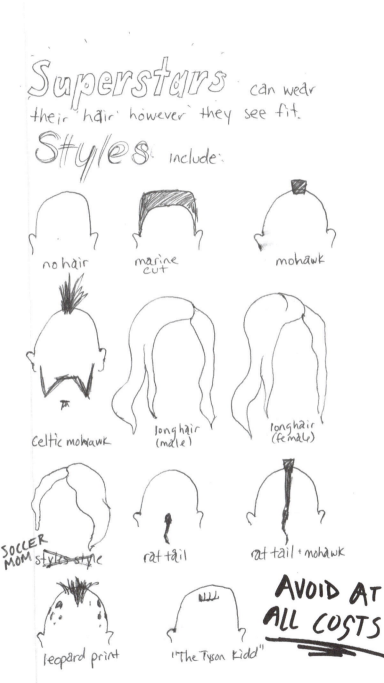

no hair

marine cut

mohawk

celtic mohawk

long hair (male)

long hair (female)

SOCCER MOM styles style

rat tail

rat tail + mohawk

leopard print

"The Tyson Kidd"

AVOID AT ALL COSTS

WORLD WRESTLING ENTERTAINMENT, INC.
1241 East Main Street, Stamford, CT 06902

Dear Mr. Venis, *AKA THE BIG VALBOWSKI*

Before you leave the backstage area for a match, please confirm with us that you are indeed wearing something under your towel. There is often concern when you're already in the ring and beginning to take it off.

Sincerely,
Talent Relations

if he doesn't obey this, his catchphrase will be, "Helllooo, Lawsuits!"

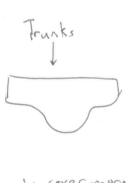

Towel

Trunks

Towels cover more than trunks....

Just saying

But what if its an Evening Gown match?

UNLESS YOU'RE THE WORLD'S LARGEST LOVE MACHINE!

RULE:
FANNY PACKS

NEW
RULE:!
NO
THEY
DON'T...

What do you
keep in there,
your dignity??

TOO BAD THIS
ISN'T 1996...

Even then....
What's next???
ZUBAZ?

Dear Mr. Mideon,

As a Superstar (and a civilized adult), you are required to wear at least some clothing at all times. A fanny pack does not count as a clothing item. Your new "naked" persona must cease, immediately.

Sincerely,
Talent Relations

But I'm finally free!

HE SHOULD BE REQUIRED TO WEAR A LOT OF CLOTHING

Right to censor was here

They could have done a better job...

IF YOU HAVE ENORMOUS BICEPS, HEADBANDS CAN BE WORN AS ARMBANDS

But shouldn't there be a limit on wristbands? He doesn't have 5 wrists.

Dear Mr. Cesaro,

Please stop ripping off your custom
suits during your entrance. We
spend many hours tailoring
these to your liking, and it's
frustrating to see you go
and destroy them immediately

"WWE Wardrobe Department

Sorry, but they
don't call me the
Swiss Superman
for nothing!

Face Paint

So long as it is not toxic,
face paint can be worn in
the ring.

When I say
"UCE," yall
say "OH!"
That's some
sweet
facepaint!

This will help
everyone
remember
the name...
GULDUST

EXPAND BEYOND
THE FACE TO
RELEASE YOUR DEMON.

WORLD WRESTLING ENTERTAINMENT, INC.
1241 East Main Street, Stamford, CT 06902

Attention Superstars,

While tattoos have always been acceptable in WWE, they are now strongly encouraged.
Corey Graves needs more guests for his WWE Network series, *Superstar Ink*.

Sincerely,
Talent Relations

if Orton is on that show,
the episode will have to
be 3 hours long...

Which does
Undertaker have
more of:
tattoos or past
'Mania opponents?

I dare Graves to
ask Brock if he
uses his chest
tat to slice
vegetables.

My client assures
you that such a foolish
remark would earn
you a one-way trip to
SUPLEX CITY

SMW

StrongMan's Warehouse

BUY 1 GET 1
50% OFF
SALE

NEVER trust a
man in a Salmon-
colored suit if he says he's
tiring — no matter how
convincing the speech
may be!

—— Think you can
just say "Never
trust a man in a
Salmon colored
Suit" Period.

For decades, many Superstars
have put just as much
energy into how they
get to the ring as they do
competing within it.

As a result, some
restrictions apply to the
pomp and circumstance
of WWE.

ENTRANCES AND EXITS

PUTTING THE "WEEEEE"
IN WWE

...ertion Superstars + Managers, to highlight the pageantry of our biggest show ever. The attached design will be your transportation to the ring for WrestleMania III.

IRAN STEAM
NUMBER 1
BOBBA!

how is Andre gonna fit in that?!

CAN WE BRING THESE BACK?

Drawn
to
Scale

Andr. →
↓cart

C. PALUMBO
AUTO DEALER
"We got wheels... and deals!"

Wanna get motors running with your entrance?
These options will accelerate your career!

Better hope
you can start it...

Motorcycle

Low Ride Convertable

No Way, ese!
Thats mine!

Superfancy/expensive Car

My Destiny

Limousine

HE'S GOT A
BICYCLE!

Ride on lawn Mower

JUAN
DEERE!

ATV

HELL YEAH

Bicycle

efficient entrances are appreciated but running to the ring at full speed is not a requirement.

WHATS UP! IS A RHETORICAL QUESTION

When making an entrance
limit posing time so
the show can proceed
on schedule
— K.D, F=VP, TP

But if you totally reek
of awesomeness, strike a
second pose for the benefit
of those w/ flash photography

Carefully nudge Orton
during his turn-buckle
pose to make sure
he doesn't get too
lost in the moment.
— Chuck

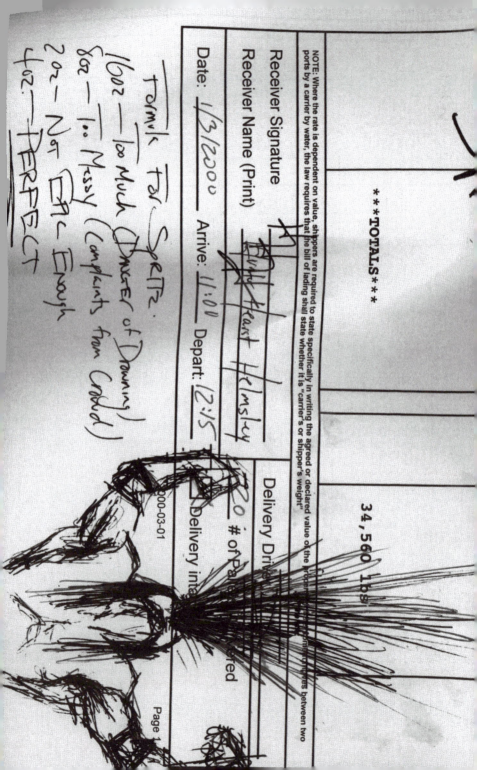

TOTALS   34,560 lbs

NOTE: Where the rate is dependent on value, shippers are required to state specifically in writing the agreed or declared value of the property. The proper punctuation is between two ports by a carrier by water, the law requires that the bill of lading shall state whether it is "carrier's or shipper's weight".

	Delivery Dri...

Receiver Signature

Receiver Name (Print)   _Living Heart Helmsley_

Date: _1/3/2000_   Arrive: _11:00_   Depart: _12:15_

000-03-01   # of Pa...   Delivery inta...   Page 1

Formula for Spritz:
16oz — Too Much (Danger of Drowning)
8oz — Too Messy (Complaints from Crowd)
2oz — Not Epic Enough
4oz — PERFECT

DELIVERY RECEIPT

Date: 1/3/2000

Ship to	Consignee				Shipment Number
Allstate Arena 6920 Mannheim Rd, Rosemont, IL 60018	Hunter Hearst Helmsley				0111751

NO. PACKAGES	DESCRIPTION	CLASS	WEIGHT		
20 pallets	16 oz. Bottled Water 72 cases per pallet		1,728 lbs		

A superstar's in EPIC! — Xaliuk

JBL's Golden Rule:
Never touch my limo
I am a wrestling GOD!

We won't Touch it, But
our crowbars + spraypaint
WILL! BROOKLYN, BROOKLYN!
—CRYME TYME

Murphy's Law
Anything that can
happen will happen.
Stone Cold's Law
Arrive.
Raise hell.
Leave.

VINCENT K. McMAHON
TITAN TOWER

A Superstar should NEVER drive a zamboni, forklift, monster truck or BEER TRUCK to the ring or any reason.

—VKM

hat about a sewage truck, ese?

What about an ~~D~~Ambulance?

8/20/01
Gang forward this same rule should apply to milk trucks as well

**National Association of
Heavy Equipment Training**
CERTIFICATE OF TRAINING

This is to certify that Steve Austin has met or exceeded the requirements of Heavy Equipment Training - Level one in the NAHETS training curriculum this twenty-eighth day of September, 1998.

Steve Cole
Steve Austin

9/28/98

And thats the bottom line 'cause the N.A.H.E.T.S. said so.

"DANGEROUS POLITICS"

BY JON HEIDENREICH

HEIDEN
HEIDENREICH
HEI-DEN-REICH

OR A

NOT a poem

POEM.

Attention WWE Superstars,

The giant fist is a decorative part of the *Smackdown* entranceway and should therefore only be viewed as such. Please simply enjoy the added boost of "ruthless aggression" it adds to your entrance. DO NOT use it as a stage for your poetry readings.

Sincerely,
Talent Relations

Michael Cole's Commentary

PLEASE.

yeah.

On Entrance Music

If a Superstar feels so
inclined, they can perform
their own entrance music.

NOTE TO ALL SUPERSTARS: leave singing to multi-talented superstars who are the BEST IN THE WORLD AT WHAT THEY DO.

STUPID IDIOTS

- Jillian Hall
- KoKo B. Ware
- R-Truth
- Shawn Michaels
- Kizarny
- Phantasio

DO YIZZOU REMIZEMBER KIZARNY?

WORLD WRESTLING ENTERTAINMENT, INC.
1241 East Main Street, Stamford, CT 06902

April 12, 2002

Dear Mr. McMahon,

Per your query, I can say with absolute certainty that no, "You Suck" is not a lyric from Kurt Angle's entrance theme.

Sincerely,
Jim Johnston

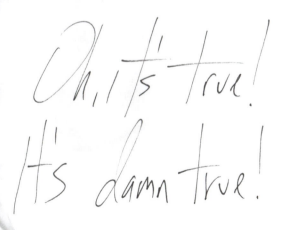

need to add some spirit to your entrance?
OUR
SQUAD
CAN
HELP!
CONTACT:
KENNY! JOHNNY!
MITCH! NICKY! MIKEY!
SERVICES INCLUDE:
-Trampolines
-Enthusiastic Cheering
-A Group of Supporters
to ~~Fire You Up!~~ beat up
OBNOXIO
YELLIN
Worked for me...
-D
very meta!
-Getting covered in ~~crap~~
Right to censor was here

WORLD WRESTLING ENTERTAINMENT, INC.
1241 East Main Street, Stamford, CT 06902

ention Superstars,

cause many of you have reported seeing them working at car dealerships across the country, we
uld like to officially state that the waving inflatable tube men used in Bayley's entrance are NOT
der exclusive contract with WWE. They are free to moonlight wherever they wish.

alent Relations

they're also really good huggers!

I ASKED ONE OF THESE GUYS 'WHATS UP?' LIKE 30 TIMES AND HE JUST STOOD THERE SMILIN' ALL WEIRD! WHATS UP WITH THAT?!
- Truth

IN CASE OF A POWER OUTAGE, LIGHT YOUR OWN WAY TO THE RING!

BORROW SOME CAMPING EQUIPMENT

DRESS LIKE A CHRISTMAS TREE

GLOW IN THE DARK

AMBROSE! YOU STILL OWE ME $17,000 YOU STUPID IDIOT!

If Bray Wyatt said it, it's probably true and false at the same time.

ENTRANCES AND
EXITS CAN
SOMETIMES OCCUR
SIMULTANEOUSLY...

KANE:
ENTERING

SETH
ROLLINS:
EXITING

CAN WE SEE YOU? NO?
THEN YOU'RE PERFECT
FOR THIS GIG!

CASTING CALL

WWE is seeking 100 men to be part of a special entrance at **WRESTLEMANIA 25.** If you fit the description below, please visit the provided website to audition. NO EXPERIENCE REQUIRED!

HO WE ARE OKING FOR

Muscular men, ages 25–35, must be close to 6'1", 250 pounds. Freestyle rapping ability a plus.

All submissions must be received by
Tuesday, March 31, 2009
We hope we "can't" see you soon!

Please allow additional time for all 100 John Cena clones to get in position on entrance ramp.
— Production Crew

WORLD WRESTLING ENTERTAINMENT, INC.
1241 East Main Street, Stamford, CT 06902

Dear Mr. Khali,

While we respect your right to express yourself during entrances, there have been in
concerns regarding the quality of your "dancing." We understand that given your m
size, you may not be as limber as smaller Superstars who have perfected the art of d
in the past. Still, it is important we help you live up to the proclamation of being "G

As a result, we are arranging for you to take ance lessons beginning next Monday
Raw. Your instructor's name is Scotty, and he plans to work with you until you're ab
perfect something called the Worm."

Sincerely,
Talent Relations

IF KHALI
WANT
DANCE
KHALI
DANCE

Even backup dancers need
a marquee-quality name...

Funkatronics
Funkadelics
Funkettes
The Funky Brunch
(Funkadactyls)

I Can Dig It!

FIREWALL

MACHINE GUN

FROM THE DESK OF

KANE

Congratulations!

If you are receiving this memo, that means you have been chosen in a random drawing to have PYRO added to your entrance. There's nothing better than blazing-hot HELLFIRE AND BRIMSTONE to strike FEAR in—ah, sorry, I got carried away there.

Anyway, please select from the following, and we can begin working with the pyrotechnics crew to create something EXPLOSIVE.

–Kane, Director of Operations

MUSHROOM CLOUD   BIG BANG

Attention Superstars,
When entering or exiting the arena through the crowd, please refrain from stealing con-
cessions from our fans in attendance.

I'm sorry
I was starving.

Sincerely,
Talent Relations

P.S. This applies to fan signs as well. Stop taking/ripping them. This is not a request.

But they gave me that beer after I finished mine! That's how SANDMAN ENTERS.

BELIEVE IN THE SHIELD's need for extra hair-wetting water on the way to the ring!

We're ready for KENNEL FROM HELL II!

Damas y caballeros,
en el camino hacia el cuadrilátero,
él es el hombre que le mete terror
a los corazones de todos sus oponentes:

¡Alberto del Río!

Anunciak!

Artículate!

And don't forget to yell!

in a Superstar has the means only can employ their ringannouncers (stooge.)

Traditional bouts often sufficed in the old days of sports-entertainment, but as rivalries intensified, so did the variety in the options for competition. Still, even matches with seemingly no rules require a few guidelines.

HEll in/on/off/through a cell

STIPULATION MATCHES

RULE
MADE
BRO

So
were
hearts

S WERE
TO BE
KEN

SO WERE
STREAKS
21-1

AND
TABLES!

RECOMMENDED HOLDS:

-SHARPSHOOTER

Double **-ANKLE LOCK**

Submission Match

No pinfalls, no count-outs   - Walls of JERICHO

The match ends when a Su-
perstar makes their opponent **YES!** Lock
tap out or verbally submit.

Triple
Threat

~~Three's Company~~/
Fatal Four Matches

Three/four Superstars compete, one fall to the
finish (pin or submission),
unless special elimination
rules apply

No disqualifications

OPTIONAL:
TEAM UP W/ ONE
GUY TO PUT THE
OTHER GUY THROUGH
THE ANNOUNCE TABLE.

If you're ever
stuck between
The Rock and a
hard place, choose
the hard place.
The Rock will
destroy you.

Battle Royal

A set number of Superstars (often 10 or 20) all begin the match at the same time. Eliminations occur when a Superstar is thrown over the top rope and both feet touch the ground.

How about the middle rope for us ladies - Moolah

No disqualifications

Superstars may exit the ring through or under the ropes and return to the ring throughout the match.

Hide until everyone else has been eliminated.

Is that Funaki?

Luckiest Numbers
#27: Most Wins (4)
#1: Most likely to last the longest

Unluckiest Numbers
#3: Most likely to be eliminated first
#9,12: Never made the final four.

If KANE is in the ring for the Royal Rumble, you'd better hope that you aren't

Royal Rumble

30 Superstars in total compete. The match begins with the participants who drew numbers 1 and 2. Every 90 seconds, a new Superstar enters the match until all 30 have entered.

Eliminations occur when a Superstar is thrown over

EXACTLY! I WAS NEVER

No disqualifications

Superstars may exit the ring through or under the ropes and return to the ring throughout the match.

The last Superstar standing after the 29 others have been eliminated is the winner.

† IN THIS!
—AXEL

It helps if you're the Chairman.
OR HIS SON-IN-LAW!

NO FAIR KISSING KHALI IN RING. KHALI DISTRACTED EASILY

NO MATTER YOUR SIZE OF SKILLS,
SURVIVE THE *ROYAL RUMBLE*
BY ANY MEANS NECESSARY.

Practice Parkour

spin

land on your hands

steal a better number, ese!

skin the cat

TV

BE REALLY BIG

Use Your Resources Well

→ Dable as Popo Stek.

BONUS TIP:
If you can set your pride aside, try lying in the fetal position and clinging to the bottom rope for dear life. You might not look like a winner, but your chances of survival will definitely go up.

THE HARDCORE
CHAMPIONSHIP
WILL NOW BE
DEFENDED
24 HOURS A DAY
7 DAYS A WEEK

WASH
YOUR
HANDS!

WORLD WRESTLING ENTERTAINMENT, INC.
1241 East Main Street, Stamford, CT 06902

Dear Mr. McMahon,

On behalf of all WWE officials, I am writing you in hopes of doing away with the 24/7 rule for the Hardcore Championship. While we understand the excitement this stipulation adds, we are finding ourselves completely exhausted trying to keep up with these on-the-spot matches. Plus, this stip has allowed for many non-Superstars to become champions, some of whom are completely unfit for WWE. Below is a list of just some of the recent Hardcore Champions:

- A popcorn vendor at MSG
- Steve Blackman's grandmother
- Ken, manager of a Chicago Holiday Inn
- A 9 year-old boy wearing an Undertaker T-shirt
- A broom that fell on Raven while he was sleeping

We hope you will understand our concerns and abolish this rule.

Sincerely,
Mike Chioda

That broom is a solid worker!

OR, you know, just get rid of the belt altogether

It's a title, you faceless bum. A belt is something you wear to keep your pants up!

Steel Cage Match

No disqualification

Win by pinfall, submission
or escaping the cage with
both feet touching the floor
on the other side.

In tag team cage matches,
tornado rules apply.
One fall to the finish for
multi-man matches.

or by getting
chokeslammed
through the
ring and
crawling out

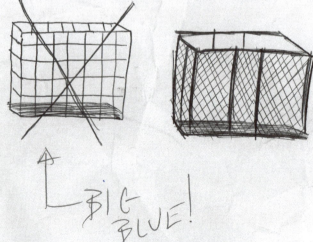

↑
└ BIG
   BLUE!

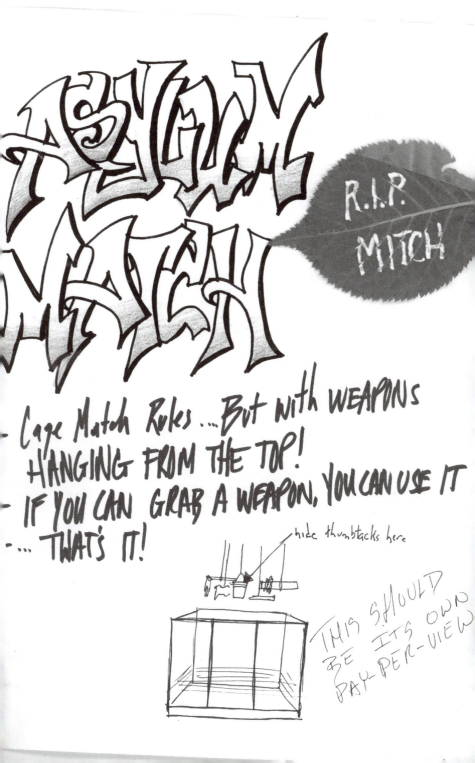

ASYLUM MATCH

R.A.P. MITCH

- Cage Match Rules ... But with WEAPONS HANGING FROM THE TOP!
- IF YOU CAN GRAB A WEAPON, YOU CAN USE IT
- ... THAT'S IT!

hide thumbtacks here

THIS SHOULD BE ITS OWN PAY-PER-VIEW

EVERY GREAT ~~STIP~~ MATCH NEEDS AN EQUALLY GREAT NICKNAME: ~~HECK~~ HELL IN A CELL

- ~~HADES' HIDEAWAY~~
- ~~BEELZEBUB'S BOX~~
- ~~LUCIFER'S LIVING ROOM~~
- ~~STEEL CAGE BUT BIGGER... WITH A ~~ROOF~~ stupid~~
- ~~TAKER'S MAN CAVE?~~
- ~~THE DEVIL'S PLAY PEN~~ close?
- THE DEVIL'S PLAYGROUND yes!
- SATAN'S STRUCTURE alliteration, yes!

MORE = CELL =

MORE HELL

new cell:

TAILLER!
HEAVIER!

Plus:
IMPOSSIBLE TO
BREAK INTO/OUT OF

Unless you're
A HOLOGRAM
HAHAHAHA!

raditional Survivor
Series Match:

Two teams of five Super- ~ Something Four
stars compete in an elimina-
tion-style tag team match.

Eliminations can occur by OR WHEN A
pinfall, submission or any VIGILANTE INTERFERES
form of DQ.

The last remaining member
of the winning team i
sole survi

well something
like a team of total rewards...

NEVER
UNDERESTIMATE
STING.

OR
ROBOCOP

you all survive!

BIG TIP:
IF YOU DON'T LIKE
YOUR PARTNERS,
JUST BEAT THEM
UP BACKSTAGE
BEFORE THE MATCH.

HOW TO WIN A STRETCHER MATCH:

1. Beat up your opponent quite a bit.

2. Put them on a stretcher

3. Push the stretcher to the finish line.

NO MATTER HOW BADLY HE'S HURT, DO NOT ASSUME MICK FOLEY WILL STAY ON THE STRETCHER. JUST DON'T.

A Dumpster Match is a great way to take out the trash.

Like Duke "The Dumpster" Droese?

Hair vs. Hair Match

Two Superstars compete in a standard rules contest.

The loser must have their head shaved.

The winner does the honors of shaving the loser's head (scissors, razors, barber chairs will be provided).

I HAVE MY OWN SHEARS!
- BRUTUS

Did Anderson and Gallows like a tag team version of this match?

Women are not exempt!

Good golly, Molly Holly, that was not a good look for you....

If you lox, you can hide your head any way you want.

WILLY'S WONDERFUL
World of
WIGS

6493 Main St. Phoenix, AZ

GREEN CLOWN	25.00
CURLY BROWN W/HEADGEAR	40.00
BLONDE STRAIGHT, LONG	30.00
MIDNIGHT BLACK, BOB	40.00
SubTotal	135.00
Total Tax	7.63
Total	142.63

Thank you, see you again soon!

VINCE "BEFORE" TRUMP

VINCE "AFTER" TRUMP

Lumberjack Match (or LUMBER JILL)

Two Superstars compete, and several Superstars surround the outside of the ring.

If a Superstar is thrown from the ring, the surrounding Superstars throw them back into the ring.

The match is only decided by pinfall or submission.

If you are serving as a lumberjack, please DO NOT bring an Ax to the ring.

GREAT WAY TO BOND WITH THE LOCKER ROOM AND/OR TAKE OUT FRUSTRATIONS

THE DOG Pen

FROM THE DESK OF

William Regal

WWE COMMISSIONER

Duchess of Queensbury Rules:

This is
for the
best.

ADVICE:
DON'T DRINK
REGAL'S TEA.
IT MIGHT ACTUALLY
BE SOMETHING
THAT RHYMES
WITH TEA...

let's

have a

BRAWL!

what

THE APA INVITATIONAL BAR ROOM BRAWL

who

YOU (IF YOU'RE MAN ENOUGH) even the Easter Bunny?

when

THIS SUNDAY AT VENGEANCE

where

A MAKESHIFT SALOON IN DENVER, CO

how

LAST MAN STANDING (AND DRINKING) WINS why?

MATCHES LIKE THIS ARE B.Y.O.B. (which, in this case, stands for "Bring Your Own Bradshaw")

or woman!
Sasha vs. Bayley

I KNOW THAT BLOKE! -OZZY

IRON MAN MATCH

Two Superstars compete for a determined amount of time (30 minutes or 60 minutes).

Whoever scores the most falls within the time limit will be the winner.

if no falls have occurred at the end of the time limit, the match goes to sudden-death overtime.

THAT'S A BUNCH OF CRAP!
- BRET

To gain an edge in this match, try arriving to the ring on a zipline

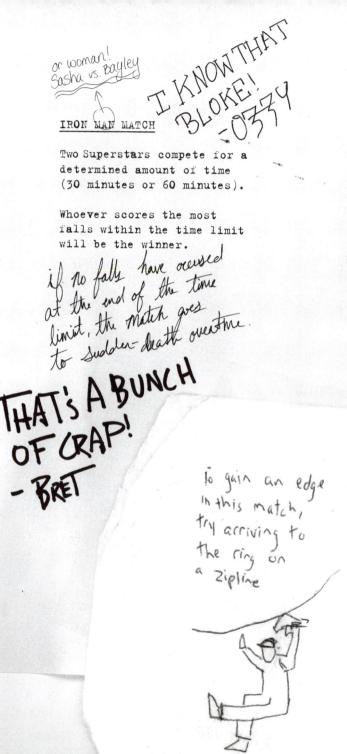

WORLD WRESTLING ENTERTAINMENT, INC.
1241 East Main Street, Stamford, CT 06902

Attention Superstars,

As referees, we feel it is our duty to answer your FAQs and clear up any confusion regarding some of the more rarely seen matches in WWE:

- A "Loser Leaves Town" match does not actually require you to move to a new residence
- There is no need to tip the driver should you lose an Ambulance Match.
- No bulls are harmed before, during or after a Texas Bullrope match.

Sincerely,
Charles Robinson

`Especially Brahma
Bull-IF YA SMELL
WHAT THE Rock
IS COOKIN'!

P.S. we're still not sure how & Punjabi Prison
match works either...

IS THAT WHY
THERE HASN'T
BEEN ANOTHER ONE?

Career-Threatening Match:

Best place to host this match: WrestleMania

Two Superstars compete
under any additional
stipulations.

The loser must retire,
unless the stipulation only
applies to one Superstar.

The retirement of the
losing Superstar must
remain permanent.

IF YOU CHALLENGE TERRY FUNK TO THIS MATCH, YOU'RE WASTING EVERYONE'S TIME

What if you challenge Chainsaw Charlie? And if he loses, does he have to bring his chainsaw to a scrap yard to retire it?

GREENER CANVAS MANOR

"Your career is over, but your life has just begun!"

ENGAGING ACTIVITIES!
Bingo | Square dancing | Jell-O | Sitting

ORGANIZED EVENTS!
Sleep | Rest | Nap time | Shut eye

EDUCATIONAL CLASSES!
How to Knit | How to Crochet | Intro to Sharing Hard Candy

Don't fade away into obscurity - try any of the following
to spend your retirement wisely:
- Send an audition tape to be cast on the next season of Legends House
- Join the pay-per-view pre-show panel **I CAN DIG THAT...SUCKA!**
- Host your own hunting show
- Relive the good times by playing as yourself in a WWE video game
- Snag that sweet GM job ⟶ Do this and you'll always HAVE A NICE DAY

THE ELIMINAT

2 MILES OF CHAIN!
10 TONS OF STEEL!

Diameter: 36ft.

← plexiglass

20ft.

4 SUPE
ENTE
AFTER
BULLET
POD OPE

16 frames
- 300 lbs each
- Black Stainless Steel

16ft.

2 SUPERSTARS
START THE
MATCH...

VERY
RELUCTANTLY

Rule of Physics
Flesh + Steel = PAINS

oft

ARS
E-BY-ONE

IR
OOF

But not
SPEAR-PROOF

or mark
Henry-proof!

ELIMINATIONS
OCCUR BY PINFALL
OR SUBMISSION.
LAST SUPERSTAR
STANDING WINS!

But even if you win
you probably won't
be standing

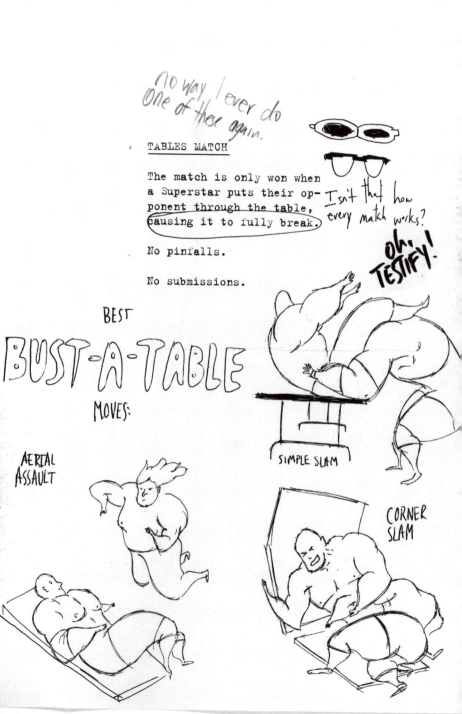

no way I ever do one of these again.

<u>TABLES MATCH</u>

The match is only won when
a Superstar puts their opponent through the table,
(causing it to fully break.)

Isn't that how every match works?

No pinfalls.

No submissions.

oh, TESTIFY!

BEST

BUST-A-TABLE

MOVES:

AERIAL
ASSAULT

SIMPLE SLAM

CORNER
SLAM

CHAIRS MATCH

During a chairs match,
Superstars are permitted
to use folding chairs to
strike their opponents on
the body. The outcome is
still determined by pinfall
or submission.

But there's no need to bury
your opponent under a
hanging tower of chairs
after you've won...

Agree to
disagree.

R Barret

IN THIS MATCH, YOUR ONLY ALLY IS THE LADDER!

LADDER MATCH

During a ladder match, the only way to win is to climb the ladder and retrieve the championship or object hanging above the ring. There are no pinfalls, submissions or disqualifications.

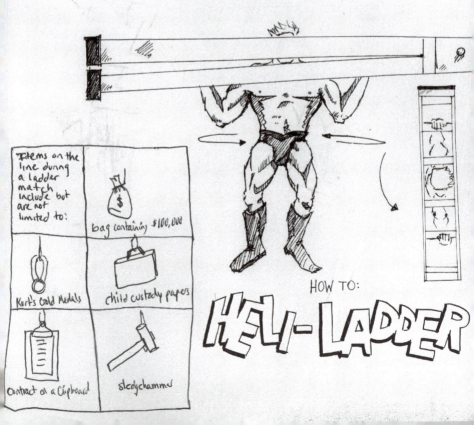

Items on the line during a ladder match include but are not limited to:

bag containing $100,000

Kurt's Gold Medals

child custody papers

Contract on a Clipboard

sledgehammer

HOW TO:

HELI-LADDER

FROM THE DESK OF
MICK FOLEY
WWE COMMISSIONER

NEW MATCH IDEA: TLC

Christian, what shall we play at the CON-CHAIR-TO Showcase?

ALL THE HITS, DUH!

During a TLC match, Superstars have tables, ladders and chairs at their disposal! Like a ladder match, the contest concludes once a Superstar is able to climb the ladder and unhook the hanging championship or object.

(does not stand for "Tender Loving Care.")

TABLES, LADDERS AND CHAIRS, OH MY!

TABLES
LADDERS
CHAIRS
+
STAIRS!

This is gonna take HBS to new heights.

before it expires. But you can cash in the right you win it.?

- The holder of the Money in the Bank briefcase can "cash in" their world title opportunity any time, any place.

- The bell must ring for a cash-in attempt to be valid.

Cashing in doesn't guarantee you a championship, though.

Right-Shadow.?

Vgh.

Pro Tip:
Don't announce your cash-in ahead of time.
Surprise Matches Rule!

~Edge

↑ WORKED FOR ME DUDE.
-RVD

This is too much, even for you, Jericho...

Money in the Bank

BAUGAU

- A briefcase containing a guaranteed WWE World — you spelled "World" wrong. Heavyweight Championship match is suspended above the ring. The Superstar who unhooks the briefcase is the winner.

AND THEY SHOULD BE CALLED IN "MR. MONEY IN THE BANK!"

Items acceptable for use in
a No Holds Barred/Hardcore/
Street Fight match include
but are not limited to:

kendo sticks
ring steps
tables
ladders
fire extinguishers
championship titles
trash cans
commentator monitors
microphones
crowbars
brass knuckles
cheese graters
baseball bats wrapped in
thumbtacks barbed wire
the ring bell
household irons
rolls of coins
car doors
flagpoles
nightsticks

road signs
baking sheets
frying pans
plumbing pipes
brooms
mops
leather belts
televisions
rotary telephones
laptop computers
encyclopedias
popcorn buckets
Slammy awards
basketballs
the kitchen sink
oars
license plates ·
light tubes
cinder blocks

- Sledge hammers
· dirty sock puppets
· acoustic guitars
Coconut
— minnequin heads
TROMBONES

*Substances/elements
acceptable for use in
"Extreme Rules" matches include but are not limited to:

salt (or other seasonings)
Kabiki powder
mysterious green mist
spewed soda
saliva
fire*
*when set to an object

EVERY SIGNATURE WEAPON NEEDS A GOOD NAME: WW

nappy

The Equalizer

BARBIE

You think that's a good name?

HEAD

HELP ME

Francesca

Last Man Standing

No disqualification, no
pinfalls, no submissions.
The match ends when one
Superstar is unable to
reach their feet before
the count of 10.

"I Quit" said John Cena, NEVER!

No disqualification,
no pinfalls

Duct Tape is
Your friend in
this Match

MAHOGANY HAVEN
CASKET COMPANY
CREATING CASKETS SINCE 1918

MODEL #037

"Old Faithful"

Interior Dimensions:
L 36" W 16" H 11"

Exterior Dimensions
L 38" W

MODEL #038

"Eternal Bliss"

Interior Dimensions:
L 34" W 14" H 9"

Exterior Dimensions
L 36" W 17" H 13"

$599.99

CASKE'T
MATCH:

Throw your opponent i
casket and close the lid.
YOU WIN.
THEY REST IN PEA

LET'S TAKE THIS
A STEP FURTHER...
BURY THEM ALIVE
TO WIN!

OR SET
CASKET ON
FIRE!

MODEL #039

"Perpetual Paradise"

Interior Dimensions:
L 28" W 10" H 12"

Exterior Dimensions
L 32" W 14" H 16"

$499.99

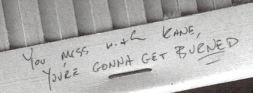

⚠ DA

BOILEF
Auth
person

NGER

ROOM

rized

el only

WWE MATCHES CAN TAKE PLACE ANYWHERE AT ANY TIME.

What about a moving truck?

-OR A MOTORCYCLE RALLY? How about the White Castle of fear??

Being a WWE Superstar is a 24/7 job. Whether they're backstage, in the parking lot or at a rival's father's funeral, a certain level of decorum is requested. And occasionally ignored.

SUPERSTAR CONDUCT

BACKSTAB HOT...

"I DON'T NEED MY HANDS TO STOMP A MUDHOLE IN YA, SON!"

WOOOO!
TIMES 3 BRO! -ZACK RYDER
YES!
RULE: SOME OF THE BEST CATCHPHRASES AREN'T "PHRASES" AT ALL
WHAT
OOOOOOH YEAH!
BANG BANG!

While we respect Superstars' right to put each other through the announce tables, we do ask that the television Monitors at least be set aside first.

—Regards
K.D., EVP, TP

Esto incluye la mesa de los locutores españoles, por favor.
—Carlos

WHAT IF THEY JUMP FROM THE TOP OL THE CELL?

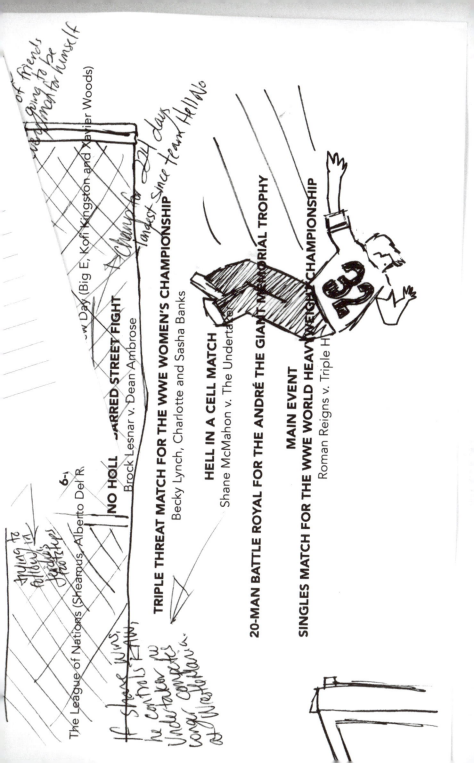

The League of Nations (Shearmus, Alberto Del R...

6-1

NO HOL... ...ARRED STREET FIGHT
Brock Lesnar v. Dean Ambrose

...w Day (Big E, Kofi Kingston and Xavier Woods)

TRIPLE THREAT MATCH FOR THE WWE WOMEN'S CHAMPIONSHIP
Becky Lynch, Charlotte and Sasha Banks

HELL IN A CELL MATCH
Shane McMahon v. The Undertaker

20-MAN BATTLE ROYAL FOR THE ANDRÉ THE GIANT MEMORIAL TROPHY

MAIN EVENT
SINGLES MATCH FOR THE WWE WORLD HEAVYWEIGHT CHAMPIONSHIP
Roman Reigns v. Triple H

trying to follow in Sheamus footsteps

If Shea wins, he contr... Undertaker longer competes at Wrestlemania

of friends ... going to be ... good mentor to himself

Champs for 24 days longest since team Hell No

Greeting cards
w/ messages like
this should not be
mailed real
on live television.

"With the deepest regrets and tears that are soaked
I'm sorry to hear that your Dad finally croaked
He lived a full life on his own terms
Soon he'll be buried and eaten by worms
But if I could have a son as stupid as you
I'd have wished for cancer so I would die too
So be brave, and be strong, get your life on track
'Cause the old bastard's DEAD
And he ain't ever comin' back!"

Flossman

← Yeah right!
Everyone knows
the Big Bossman
can't read
or write!

Superstars should not show up uninvited to the funeral of a rival's loved one. And they DEFINITELY should NOT abscond with the remains!

Celebrating a Life

IN LOVING MEMORY

Paul Randall Wight Sr.
April 8, 1944–November 11, 1999

"You were a big man. Your son is even bigger. But your ~~heart~~ butt is the biggest of all."

HAHAHAHAHA

WORLD WRESTLING ENTERTAINMENT, INC.
1241 East Main Street, Stamford, CT 06902

Attention Superstars,

On the following pages of this packet, you will find a running list of offenses that could lead to hearing Mr. McMahon yell "YOU'RE FIRED!" Many of the actions listed may seem unusually specific, but that is because they have already been committed by former Superstars. AND STAF

Please be advised that what you are about to read may be lewd/offensive/disturbing/explicit. We hope you will learn from history and not repeat these mistakes.

Best,
Talent Relations

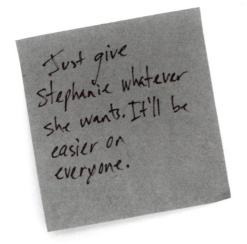

Just give Stephanie whatever she wants. It'll be easier on everyone.

And a valet in Reno.

3:16
"I "just" ~~pissed~~
my "pants"

Right to
center was
here.

October 20, 1998

Attention All Superstars:

While WWE will always respect the rights granted to you by the Second Amendment of the Constitution, Superstars are expressly forbidden from bringing firearms into the ring. This policy is non-negotiable, and anyone in violation of it will be dealt with accordingly.

Please note: This policy extends to novelty weapons that appear to be authentic firearms.

VKM

dictated not read

What if we warn you
ahead of time so
you can buy diapers first?

BANG!
3:16

Remember
Pillman 9mm?

actual hair from Luke Harper's beard. DO NOT EAT!

Gonna use
Rubber bands.
Thanks!
—Captain Lou

On The Subject of Beards

Beards are allowed provided
they are ~~well kempt~~ and do
not extend farther than 3
inches below the ~~chin~~. ANKLE

GOATEES CAN VARY
BY or be named for a SUPERSTAR

~~Hunter~~
the
game

V

W the
fuji

the
anvil

Things I found in
Bray Wyatt's beard:
- Gum
- A clothespin
- One baby alligator
- Keys to an airboat
- A smaller beard

I mention this because I think
he should be required to shave it,

OR AT LEAST WASH IT.

HELP THIS FRESH-FACED YOUNG MAN BECOME A WWE CHAMPION

DRAW A BEARD ON DANIEL BRYAN

A
Superstar
should have an
ELECTRIFYING
facial gesture

(o o)
Flaring Nostril

Licking Chin

Wiggle Ears

failed I only
have one ear
to wiggle
Foley

Raising an Eyebrow

THE Rock says this will
ELECTRIFY millions... AND MILLIONS

DEADLY PETS
WAREHOUSE

8/25/91   17:54:13

                              QTY
                               1

COBRA   949.99
                            78.29

SUBTOTAL
TOTAL TAX   1028.28

              TOTAL   1028.28
              TENDER   1100.00
              CHANGE   71.72

****
***** No Exchange or Refunds
****

to

Mone

A COBRA
WEDDING

why? Did you registe

The lovely Miss Elizabeth
and
...cho Man Randy Savage
...the honour of your presence
...at their wedding
...in the middle of the ring
at
...on Square Garden
...ght, August 26, 1991

Oh Yeah!
...NOT AN APPROPRIATE
...IFT

...the Python instead?

So long as they maintain journalist
their own talk shows.

and utter disappointments

• Can you take a punch/Are you ready to find out?

• What's that on your shirt? (NOTE: point to their shirt, when they look down, pop them across the nose. No need for a follow up here.)

• True or False: You're much dumber than you look.

• How do you expect to win matches when you're such a loser?

• How do you feel about having a coconut smashed on your head?

(NOTE: whenever it seems like they know the answers, feel free to change the questions)

Do you know where I could get some bubble gum? I'm all out...

integrity, Superstars can host

NITTER'S NITE

Possible Guests: Andre the Giant Oaf
Ricky "in Drag'in" Steamboat
Stupidfly Jimmy Snooks

Formerly
nice car

Cement

STONE
COLD

Vince

The only thing
accurate here
are the tears.

LUXURY GOODS
INSURANCE CORP

3208 Millionaire Mile
New York, NY 10304

October 13, 1998

Dear Mr. McMahon,

We have reviewed your claim thoroughly and are afraid there is no clause in your insurance policy that covers your Corvette being filled with cement. Particularly given that you were parked so close to that construction zone. If anything, we could try to classify this incident as an act of God, but as far as we can tell, Stone Cold Steve Austin isn't God—he's just very good at being bad.

We hope you understand.

Sincere

All WWE Superstars and executives should park their personal vehicles in designated zones and parking lots or garages in the arena area. Bad stuff might happen otherwise.

—Lem K, Safety Director

WE CATERING

STARTERS AND

...d Salad
...ed Salad
...pinach Salad
...Salad
...o
...Fingers
...latter
...Veggies
...er
...ngs
...es

ENTREES

...ken
...migiana
... Peppers

...oli
...dka
...mon
...ine

DESSERTS

...Cookies
...Cookies
...Cake

...ream Cake

Dear Superstars, and crew,
    While we appreciate the cultural diversity
each member of the team contributes to the
overall atmosphere backstage, the catering
crew respectfully asks that worms or any
other nontraditional "foods" that could
disturb the appetites of other Superstars be
consumed outside of the catering area.
We, and our stomachs, thank you.
        —Chef Kimmy
        WWE Catering

This includes large
moles growing on
someone's face.
↑
should also
include Tommy
Dreamer's hair.

It's my hair.
I can eat it
if I want.

WORLD WRESTLING ENTERTAINMENT, INC.
1241 East Main Street, Stamford, CT 06902

~~To Whom It May Concern,~~ *Rikishi*

I'M NOT that big, brudda

While the fact that we must send this memo again is disturbing in and of itself, there have been a number of complaints, and we must therefore address the elephant in the room.

Please refrain from purposefully flatulating upon one another during a match. The WWE ring is a place to prove one's athletic and strategic prowess—not to expel your intestinal ga in the hopes that it will debilitate your opponent. While it is difficult to prove unequivoca who "dealt it," during a match we can all certainly smell it—and there will be repercussion if these incidents continue to be overt.

Additionally, while it may prove popular with the crowd, it is unbecoming for a Superstar to rub, mash, press or shake their buttocks on, against or into the face(s) of anyone in the ring*—particularly when they are in a prone/vulnerable state.

This is our fourth specific mention of this topic. We hope it will be our last. ● ● *I did it for The Rock*

—Talent Relations

We can smell it from the announce table. Booker T threw up on me after being in the ring with that monster. PLEASE, Make it stop.

└── This is the first time I have ever agreed with Michael Cole.

* GUESS THIS DOESN'T APPLY TO VINCE OR THE KISS MY ▬▬ CLUB??

[Right to Censor was here]

Dear Superstar,

We know you're joking, but the following ~~friends~~ items will Never be on the menu so PLEASE STOP asking for them:

- Cross Face Chicken Wings
- Butt Butts Buttcakes
- Candy Asses ⟵ — — — who would want that?

— WWE Catering

...ass with small lacerations ... Orton because he was covered in bits of
he above through the window of Mr.'s own ... That would be ... and it's doubtful
the scene myself and my partner found Mr. H assaulting Mr. Orton. When I arrived on
ed to restrain Mr. ... but he is ... I'll admit, a big dude. We eventually cuffed
Mr. H and booked him. Upon further questioning, Mr. Orton revealed he had been
antagonizing Mr. H, a former work colleague, before the incident happened,
but he admits he felt he was doing so from the safety of his own home and had
assumed Mr. H was at an area many miles away for a live television taping.
After handcuffing Mr. H, officers assessed damages done to Mr. Orton and his
property. Along with physical abrasions, Mr. Orton also claims to have experi-
enced emotional trauma. Mr. Orton asked us to witness the damages to his home
as a result of the fight, but we cannot confirm how much, if any, of this damage
was caused by the brawl itself. It looks like the kind of guy who might punch
a hole in his own wall, so there's no way to know what damages might have already occurred before Mr. H arrived.

DAMAGES

Front door = $400
Wall art/family photos = $35
Tri-fold door, kicked in = $165
Large bookshelf knocked over = $205 plus associated book replacement fees, est. $148
Wall dented in the shape of a man's forehead = $215
Tall black shelf lamp crushed under Orton = $105
Shattered large window sash = $765

Total cost of damages = $2,038

[handwritten annotations:] SHOW UP AT ANOTHER'S HOUSE UNINVITED

Orton got barbershopped!

Pride = $1000?

MISSOURI
STATE POLICE
DEPARTMENT

INCIDENT REPORT

DATE OF EVENT	LOCATION
March 9, 2009	Randy Orton's House

SECTION I.

CASE NUMBER
2004800000005A

INJURED PARTY
Randy Orton

ADDRESS

PHONE NUMBER

SECTION II.

SUSPECT
Paul "Triple H" Levesque

SEX	HEIGHT	WEIGHT	DATE OF BIRTH
Male	6'4"	2__	7/27/69

| | | | EYES Filled with rage; brown? |

INCIDENT

At 9:56 p.m on Monday, March 9, I received a call from the neighbors of Randall Keith Orton who reported a suspicious man on the premises described as a "greasy-haired Sean Bean". The man was armed with a sledgehammer and wore a black leather jacket. Based on eyewitness accounts, the assailant broke down the front door with his sledgehammer before swinging the...

WAIVER AND RELEASE OF LIABILITY

In consideration of the risk of injury while particip...
"Activity"), and as conside...
heirs

FROM THE DESK OF

VINCENT K. McMAHON
TITAN TOWER

Dear Ashton Kutcher,

We're thrilled you're here.

Please take caution when appearing on WWE television. WWE is a live show unlike any other, and you won't be able to hide behind extra takes or some director mouthing words to you off camera. Good actually. But they may not actually be You're on your own. If you have bodyguards, that's fine. Good actually. But they may not actually be able to help you. Just saying.

We cannot guarantee any WWE Superstar will not grow agitated or frustrated and will possibly at-tempt to confront you inside the ring. This is a formal warning. Good luck and have fun! And protect JON yourself at all times, obviously. *Just ask Drew Carey. or Freddie Prinze Jr.! OR JON STEV*

Please see the attached waiver absolving WWE of any responsibility should you ~~MOOTH OF~~
~~TO THE WRONG GUY AND GET PUT IN YOUR PLACE!~~

—VKM

Dictated not read.

Dear Talent Relations,

I feel thorough background checks should be conducted for new Superstars to make sure they aren't Stalkers/creepy obsessed fans. I think you know who I'm reffering to...

somehow The Stalker got hired...

— Trish

Trish!!!
OMG Trish!!!
I love you!!!

Always guarantee 100% STRATUSFACTION.

TRIPLE H
WITH STEPHANIE McMAHON
What about Hornswoggle??
"LIKE FATHER, LIKE SON" TAG TEAM MATCH
RANDY ORTON and "COWBOY" BOB ORTON
vs
THE ROCK and ROCKY JOHNSON
THE UNDERTAKER
vs
KANE
half siblings count?
OHHH YESSS!
Why not a Intercontinental Championship Match? Bella v. Bella?
"THE COUSINS" HARDCORE MATCH
HARDCORE HOLLY vs CRASH HOLLY
JEFF HARDY vs MATT HARDY
WINNER BECOMES A HARDY MAN
what if your child is a rubber hand?
TREAT FAMILY MEMBERS THE WAY YOU'D TREAT ANY OTHER

FAMILY FEST

presents

MAIN EVENT
TRIPLE THREAT FOR CONTROL OF WWE

MR. McMAHON

vs

SHANE

What about Linda? Because this is basically a real marriage...

POSSIBLE TEAM NAME? THE ROCK...

Guest Commentary

At the Chairman or GM's request, Superstars are permitted to call matches alongside regular commentary contributors from ringside at the announce table provided they are fair, balanced and not a danger to themselves or those in the ring.

It should be noted that the opportunity to work as a guest commentator is a privilege, not a right. Don't squander it.

Mr. Perfect is perfect at everything he does — including commentary!

Other skills at which Mr. Perfect Excels:
- Basketball
- Bowling a perfect game
- Hitting home runs (perfectly)
- Ping Pong
- Throwing the perfect touchdown pass (then catching it)
- Horseshoe
- Shoeing horses
- Playing goalie (soccer or hockey)
- Darts
- Billiards (8 or 9 ball)
- Putting and Driving (Golf or cars)
- Making lists
- Cooking

-LOSING HIS INTERCONTINEN
CHAMPIONSHIP
TO THE HITMA

Notable exception from this list?
Handwriting

ruining someone else's match!

Ziggler's Guide to guest Commentary

• Talking about the match is not as important as talking about yourself.

• If you're going to talk about your rival, make sure what you're saying is insulting

• Show OFF your best blazer

• ~~Wear Pink~~   *no problem* -nattie

• If you do stand-up comedy on the side, use this time to try out some new material.

• Never stay on ~~commentary~~ commentary for an entire match— seize any opportunity to ditch the headset and cost your rival the win.

How's your stand-up career going?

Well, I'm sitting down right now...

WORLD WRESTLING ENTERTAINMENT, INC.
1241 East Main Street, Stamford, CT 06902

January 10, 2006 ~~Rated~~ R

Attention Superstars,

Please be advised that celebrations involving explicit public displays of affection are completely inappropriate for a WWE ring.

Sincerely,
Talent Relations PRUDES

PLEASE BE A RATED-~~PG~~ SUPERSTAR

"For the benefit of those with night vision photography..."

SURVIVOR
SERIES

John Cena vs. Team Authority

t it be known that on this date, November 17, 2014, in the town of Roanoke, Virginia, USA, the
nting of a WWE contract was finalized, and this contract was distributed for review to the under-
ned members of Team Cena and Team Authority. Their match will take place at the *Survivor Series*
the Scottrade Center in the city of San Francisco, California, USA, on December 1, 2014.

ALWAYS MAKE SURE YOUR CONTRACT SIGNING ENDS IN CHAOS.

AME _____ DATE _____

IGNATURE _____

IGNATURE _____

WITNESS _____

WITNESS _____

*WWE CONTRACT
Signing DOs and DON'Ts*

DO
- Use the contract signing to browbeat *OR JUST BEAT UP* your opponent
- Bring backup
- Toss the chairs aside to show you're ready to fight
- Angrily flip the table or put your opponent through it. *OR BOTH*

DON'T
- Flinch first during stare down
- Shake your opponent's hand → *unless you wanna get flipped onto their shoulder for a brutal finish*
- Ignore the fine print. You could end up *losing more than your title.*
- Forget to, you know, sign the contract.

Dear Superstars,

Winning the Money in the Bank contract guarantees you the opportunity to challenge for the WWE World Heavyweight Championship at any time. It does not, however, grant you immunity with regard to using the briefcase that contains the contract as a weapon. Assaulting anyone with the briefcase within the confines of a match is grounds for disqualification.

As a side note, you technically don't need to carry the briefcase around. The contract is inside. It's a piece of paper. A briefcase is not a contract.

Fig. A: This is the Money in the Bank briefcase

Fig. B: This is the contract within the Money in the Bank briefcase

—Talent Relations

What about Mr.Kennedy

Who?

Is that
BBQ SAUCE?

BOOMER SOONER

Vince,

What a Slobberknocker!
Hey, can we make it so these guys only
have one name? I'm gettin' confused out
there at the announcer table. I swear
I saw the same guy enter the
Rumble three times tonight.

— JR

HELLO my name is Sock i

MANKIND

HELLOVE my name is

DUDE LOVE

HELLO my name is

CACTUS JACK

Vickie Guerrero
General Manager of Smackdown!

What if they're anonymous?

Hello,

All WWE Superstars must treat general managers with respect!!! As general manager of *Smackdown* it is my position that arguing with decisions and name calling are absolutely unacceptable!!!

—Vickie Guerrero
General Manager of Smackdown

You forgot to mention you're the general manager of Smackdown...

Excuse ME

The enemy of your enemy is your friend.

Unless you hate them even more

From the Desk of

Stephanie McMahon

Chief Brand Officer of WWE

April 3, 2016

Attention All Superstars,

As many of you may know, there is a revolution happening with not just the women in WWE, but in all sports. And because the women of WWE are just as valuable and exciting as the men, I would like to formally declare that going forward, all WWE talent will now be referred to as Superstars. The term "Diva" is officially retired. *Unless referring to The Miz*

Subsequently, the women's triple threat match tonight will be for the brand new WWE Women's Championship.

Sincerely,
Stephanie McMahon

Either way I'm still a 100% LASS KICKER

BYE BYE, BUTTERFLY

← OLD & BUSTED

↙ NEW HOTNESS!

Achievement

ify that

MORE

More like
Enzo A. Moron...
-KO

Y A G. *And a hip-hop hobbit.*

STUD,

RULE

YOU CAN'T
TEACH THAT!

Form **1040**

Department of the Treasury—Internal Revenue Service

U.S. Individual Income Tax Return **1991**

For the year Jan.–Dec. 31, 1991, or other tax year beginning , 1991, ending , 19   OMB No. 1545-0074

Label
(See instructions on page 11.)

Use the IRS label. Otherwise, please print or type.

L A B E L   H E R E

Your first name and initial | Last name | Your social security number

If a joint return, spouse's first name and initial | Last name | Spouse's social security number

Home address (number and street). (If you have a P.O. box, see page 11.) | Apt. no.

City, town or post office, state, and ZIP code. (If you have a foreign address, see page 11.)

For Privacy Act and Paperwork Reduction Act Notice, see instructions.

Presidential Election Campaign
(See page 11.)

▶ Do you want $1 to go to this fund? ☐ Yes ☐ No

If joint return, does your spouse want $1 to go to this fund? ☐ Yes ☐ No

Note: Checking "Yes" will not change your tax or reduce your refund.

Filing Status

Check only one box.

1 ☐ Single
2 ☐ Married filing joint return (even if only one had income)
3 ☐ Married filing separate return. Enter spouse's social security no. above and full name here. ▶
4 ☐ Head of household (with qualifying person). (See page 12.) If the qualifying person is a child but not your dependent, enter this child's name here. ▶
5 ☐ Qualifying widow(er) with dependent child (year spouse died ▶ 19   ). (See page 12.)

Exemptions
(See page 12.)

6a ☐ Yourself. If your parent (or someone else) can claim you as a dependent on his or her tax return, do not check box 6a. But be sure to check the box on line 33b on page 2

b ☐ Spouse

c Dependents:

(1) Name (first, initial, and last name)	(2) Check if under age 1	(3) If age 1 or older, dependent's social security number	(4) Dependent's relationship to you	(5) No. of months lived in your home in 1991

If more than six dependents, see page 13.

No. of boxes checked on 6a and 6b

No. of your children on 6c who:
• lived with you
• didn't live with you due to divorce or separation (see page 14)

No. of other dependents on 6c

d If your child didn't live with you but is claimed as your dependent under a pre-1985 agreement, check here ▶ ☐
e Total number of exemptions claimed

Add numbers entered on lines above ▶

Income

Attach Copy B of your Forms W-2, W-2G, and 1099-R here.

If you did not get a W-2, see page 10.

Attach check or money order on top of any Forms W-2, W-2G, or 1099-R.

7 Wages, salaries, tips, etc. (attach Form(s) W-2) | 7
8a Taxable interest income (also attach Schedule B if over $400) | 8a
b Tax-exempt interest income (see page 16). DON'T include on line 8a | 8b
9 Dividend income (also attach Schedule B if over $400) | 9
10 Taxable refunds of state and local income taxes, if any, from worksheet on page 16 | 10
11 Alimony received | 11
12 Business income or (loss) (attach Schedule C) | 12
13 Capital gain or (loss) (attach Schedule D) | 13
14 Capital gain distributions not reported on line 13 (see page 17) | 14
15 Other gains or (losses) (attach Form 4797) | 15
16a Total IRA distributions | 16a | 16b Taxable amount (see page 17) | 16b
17a Total pensions and annuities | 17a | 17b Taxable amount (see page 17) | 17b
18 Rents, royalties, partnerships, estates, trusts, etc. (attach Schedule E) | 18
19 Farm income or (loss) (attach Schedule F) | 19
20 Unemployment compensation (insurance) (see page 18) | 20
21a Social security benefits | 21a | 21b Taxable amount (see page 18) | 21b
22 Other income (list type and amount—see page 19) | 22
23 Add the amounts shown in the far right column for lines 7 through 22. This is your **total income** ▶ | 23

Adjustments to Income

(See page 19.)

24a Your IRA deduction, from applicable worksheet on page 20 or 21 | 24a
b Spouse's IRA deduction, from applicable worksheet on page 20 or 21 | 24b
25 One-half of self-employment tax (see page 21) | 25
26 Self-employed health insurance deduction, from worksheet on page 22 | 26
27 Keogh retirement plan and self-employed SEP deduction | 27
28 Penalty on early withdrawal of savings | 28
29 Alimony paid. Recipient's SSN ▶ | 29
30 Add lines 24a through 29. These are your **total adjustments** ▶ | 30

Adjusted Gross Income

31 Subtract line 30 from line 23. This is your **adjusted gross income**. If this amount is less than $21,250 and a child lived with you, see page 45 to find out if you can claim the "Earned Income Credit" on line 56. ▶ | 31

Cat. No. 11320B